MEDIEVAL CASTLES

Titles in the Series
Greenwood Guides to Historic Events of the Medieval World

The Black Death

The Crusades

Eleanor of Aquitaine, Courtly Love, and the Troubadours

Genghis Khan and Mongol Rule

Joan of Arc and the Hundred Years War

Magna Carta

Medieval Castles

Medieval Cathedrals

The Medieval City

Medieval Science and Technology

The Puebloan Society of Chaco Canyon

The Rise of Islam

MEDIEVAL CASTLES

Marilyn Stokstad

Greenwood Guides to Historic Events of the Medieval World
Jane Chance, Series Editor

GREENWOOD PRESS
Westport, Connecticut • London

Library of Congress Cataloging-in-Publication Data

Stokstad, Marilyn, 1929–
  Medieval castles / Marilyn Stokstad.
      p. cm. — (Greenwood guides to historic events of the medieval world)
    Includes bibliographical references and index.
    ISBN 0–313–32525–1 (alk. paper)
    1. Castles—Great Britain.   2. Castles—France.   I. Title.   II. Series.
  UG429.G7S76   2005
  355.7'094'0902—dc22   2004028450

British Library Cataloguing in Publication Data is available.

Library of Congress Catalog Card Number: 2004028450
ISBN: 0–313–32525–1

First published in 2005

Greenwood Press, 88 Post Road West, Westport, CT 06881
An imprint of Greenwood Publishing Group, Inc.
www.greenwood.com

Printed in the United States of America

The paper used in this book complies with the
Permanent Paper Standard issued by the National
Information Standards Organization (Z39.48–1984).

10 9 8 7 6 5 4 3 2 1

CONTENTS

ILLUSTRATIONS

SERIES FOREWORD

The Middle Ages are no longer considered the "Dark Ages" (as Petrarch termed them), sandwiched between the two enlightened periods of classical antiquity and the Renaissance. Often defined as a historical period lasting, roughly, from 500 to 1500 C.E., the Middle Ages span an enormous amount of time (if we consider the way other time periods have been constructed by historians) as well as an astonishing range of countries and regions very different from one another. That is, we call the "Middle" Ages the period beginning with the fall of the Roman Empire as a result of raids by northern European tribes of "barbarians" in the late antiquity of the fifth and sixth centuries and continuing until the advent of the so-called Italian and English renaissances, or rebirths of classical learning, in the fifteenth and sixteenth centuries. How this age could be termed either "Middle" or "Dark" is a mystery to those who study it. Certainly it is no longer understood as embracing merely the classical inheritance in the west or excluding eastern Europe, the Middle East, Asia, or even, as I would argue, North and Central America.

Whatever the arbitrary, archaic, and hegemonic limitations of these temporal parameters—the old-fashioned approach to them was that they were mainly not classical antiquity, and therefore not important—the Middle Ages represent a time when certain events occurred that have continued to affect modern cultures and that also, inevitably, catalyzed other medieval events. Among other important events, the Middle Ages saw the birth of Muhammad (c. 570–632) and his foundation of Islam in the seventh century as a rejection of Christianity which led to the imperial conflict between East and West in the eleventh and twelfth centuries. In western Europe in the Middle Ages the foundations for modern nationalism and modern law were laid and the concept of romantic love arose in the Middle Ages, this latter event partly one of the indirect consequences of the Crusades. With the shaping of national identity came the need to defend boundaries against invasion; so the castle emerged as a military outpost—whether in northern Africa, during the Crusades, or in Wales, in the eleventh century, to defend William of Normandy's newly acquired provinces—to satisfy that need. From Asia the invasions of Genghis Khan changed the literal and cultural shape of eastern and southern Europe.

In addition to triggering the development of the concept of chivalry and the knight, the Crusades influenced the European concepts of the lyric, music, and musical instruments; introduced to Europe an appetite for spices like cinnamon, coriander, and saffron and for dried fruits like prunes and figs as well as a desire for fabrics such as silk; and brought Aristotle to the European university through Arabic and then Latin translations. As a result of study of the "new" Aristotle, science and philosophy dramatically changed direction—and their emphasis on this material world helped to undermine the power of the Catholic Church as a monolithic institution in the thirteenth century.

By the twelfth century, with the centralization of the one (Catholic) Church, came a new architecture for the cathedral—the Gothic—to replace the older Romanesque architecture and thereby to manifest the Church's role in the community in a material way as well as in spiritual and political ways. Also from the cathedral as an institution and its need to dramatize the symbolic events of the liturgy came medieval drama—the mystery and the morality play, from which modern drama derives in large part. Out of the cathedral and its schools to train new priests (formerly handled by monasteries) emerged the medieval institution of the university. Around the same time, the community known as a town rose up in eastern and western Europe as a consequence of trade and the necessity for a new economic center to accompany the development of a bourgeoisie, or middle class. Because of the town's existence, the need for an itinerant mendicancy that could preach the teachings of the Church and beg for alms in urban centers sprang up.

Elsewhere in the world, in North America the eleventh-century settlement of Chaco Canyon by the Pueblo peoples created a social model like no other, one centered on ritual and ceremony in which the "priests" were key, but one that lasted barely two hundred years before it collapsed and its central structures were abandoned.

In addition to their influence on the development of central features of modern culture, the Middle Ages have long fascinated the modern age because of parallels that exist between the two periods. In both, terrible wars devastated whole nations and peoples; in both, incurable diseases plagued cities and killed large percentages of the world's population. In both periods, dramatic social and cultural changes took place as a result of these events: marginalized and overtaxed groups in societies rebelled against imperious governments; trade and a burgeoning middle class came to the fore; outside the privacy of the family, women began to have a greater role in Western societies and their cultures.

How different cultures of that age grappled with such historical change is the subject of the Greenwood Guides to Historic Events of the Medieval World. This series features individual volumes that illuminate key events in medieval world history. In some cases, an "event" occurred during a relatively limited time period. The troubadour lyric as a phenomenon, for example, flowered and died in the courts of Aquitaine in the twelfth century, as did the courtly romance in northern Europe a few decades later. The Hundred Years War between France and England generally took place during a precise time period, from the fourteenth to mid-fifteenth centuries.

In other cases, the event may have lasted for centuries before it played itself out: the medieval Gothic cathedral, for example, may have been first built in the twelfth century at Saint-Denis in Paris (c. 1140), but cathedrals, often of a slightly different style of Gothic architecture, were still being built in the fifteenth century all over Europe and, again, as the symbolic representation of a bishop's seat, or chair, are still being built today. And the medieval city, whatever its incarnation in the early Middle Ages, basically blossomed between the eleventh and thirteenth centuries as a result of social, economic, and cultural changes. Events—beyond a single dramatic historically limited happening—took longer to affect societies in the Middle Ages because of the lack of political and social centralization, the primarily agricultural and rural nature of most countries, difficulties in communication, and the distances between important cultural centers.

Each volume includes necessary tools for understanding such key events in the Middle Ages. Because of the postmodern critique of authority that modern societies underwent at the end of the twentieth century, students and scholars as well as general readers have come to mistrust the commentary and expertise of any one individual scholar or commentator and to identify the text as an arbiter of "history." For this reason, each book in the series can be described as a "library in a book." The intent of the series is to provide a quick, in-depth examination and current perspectives on the event to stimulate critical thinking as well as ready-reference materials, including primary documents and biographies of key individuals, for additional research.

Specifically, in addition to a narrative historical overview that places the specific event within the larger context of a contemporary perspective, five to seven developmental chapters explore related focused aspects of the event. In addition, each volume begins with a brief chronology and ends with a conclusion that discusses the consequences and impact of the event. There are also brief biographies of twelve to twenty key individuals (or places or buildings, in the book on the cathedral); primary documents from the period (for example, letters, chronicles, memoirs, diaries, and other writings) that illustrate states of mind or the turn of events at the time, whether historical, literary, scientific, or philosophical; illustrations (maps, diagrams, manuscript illuminations, portraits); a glossary of terms; and an annotated bibliography of important books, articles, films, and CD-ROMs available for additional research. An index concludes each volume.

No particular theoretical approach or historical perspective characterizes the series; authors developed their topics as they chose, generally taking into account the latest thinking on any particular event. The editors selected final topics from a list provided by an advisory board of high school teachers and public and school librarians. On the basis of nominations of scholars made by distinguished writers, the series editor also tapped internationally known scholars, both those with lifelong expertise and others with fresh new perspectives on a topic, to author the twelve books in the series. Finally, the series editor selected distinguished medievalists, art historians, and archaeologists to complete an advisory board: Gwinn Vivian, retired professor of archaeology at the University of Arizona Museum; Sharon Kinoshita, associate professor of French literature, world literature, and cultural studies at the University of California–Santa Cruz; Nancy Wu, associate museum educator at the Metropolitan Museum of Art, The Cloisters, New York City; and Christo-

pher A. Snyder, chair of the Department of History and Politics at Mary-
mount University.

In addition to examining the event and its effects on the specific cultures involved through an array of documents and an overview, each volume provides a new approach to understanding these twelve events.
Treated in the series are: the Black Death; the Crusades; Eleanor of
Aquitaine, courtly love, and the troubadours; Genghis Khan and Mongol rule; Joan of Arc and the Hundred Years War; Magna Carta; the medieval castle, from the eleventh to the sixteenth centuries; the medieval
cathedral; the medieval city, especially in the thirteenth century; medieval science and technology; Muhammad and the rise of Islam; and the
Puebloan society of Chaco Canyon.

The Black Death, by Joseph Byrne, isolates the event of the epidemic
of bubonic plague in 1347–52 as having had a signal impact on medieval
Europe. It was, however, only the first of many related such episodes involving variations of pneumonic and septicemic plague that recurred over
350 years. Taking a twofold approach to the Black Death, Byrne investigates both the modern research on bubonic plague, its origins and
spread, and also medieval documentation and illustration in diaries, artistic works, and scientific and religious accounts. The demographic, economic, and political effects of the Black Death are traced in one chapter,
the social and psychological patterns of life in another, and cultural expressions in art and ritual in a third. Finally, Byrne investigates why
bubonic plague disappeared and why we continue to be fascinated by it.
Documents included provide a variety of medieval accounts—Byzantine,
Arabic, French, German, English, and Italian—several of which are
translated for the first time.

The Crusades, by Helen Nicholson, presents a balanced account of various crusades, or military campaigns, invented by Catholic or "Latin"
Christians during the Middle Ages against those they perceived as threats
to their faith. Such expeditions included the Crusades to the Holy Land
between 1095 and 1291, expeditions to the Iberian Peninsula, the "crusade" to northeastern Europe, the Albigensian Crusades and the Hussite
crusades—both against the heretics—and the crusades against the Ot-
toman Turks (in the Balkans). Although Muslim rulers included the concept of jihâd (a conflict fought for God against evil or his enemies) in
their wars in the early centuries of Islam, it had become less important
in the late tenth century. It was not until the middle decades of the

twelfth century that jihâd was revived in the wars with the Latin Christian Crusaders. Most of the Crusades did not result in victory for the Latin Christians, although Nicholson concedes they slowed the advance of Islam. After Jerusalem was destroyed in 1291, Muslim rulers did permit Christian pilgrims to travel to holy sites. In the Iberian Peninsula, Christian rulers replaced Muslim rulers, but Muslims, Jews, and dissident Christians were compelled to convert to Catholicism. In northeastern Europe, the Teutonic Order's campaigns allowed German colonization that later encouraged twentieth-century German claims to land and led to two world wars. The Albigensian Crusade wiped out thirteenth-century aristocratic families in southern France who held to the Cathar heresy, but the Hussite crusades in the 1420s failed to eliminate the Hussite heresy. As a result of the wars, however, many positive changes occurred: Arab learning founded on Greek scholarship entered western Europe through the acquisition of an extensive library in Toledo, Spain, in 1085; works of western European literature were inspired by the holy wars; trade was encouraged and with it the demand for certain products; and a more favorable image of Muslim men and women was fostered by the crusaders' contact with the Middle East. Nicholson also notes that America may have been discovered because Christopher Columbus avoided a route that had been closed by Muslim conquests and that the Reformation may have been advanced because Martin Luther protested against the crusader indulgence in his Ninety-five Theses (1517).

Eleanor of Aquitaine, Courtly Love, and the Troubadours, by ffiona Swabey, singles out the twelfth century as the age of the individual, in which a queen like Eleanor of Aquitaine could influence the development of a new social and artistic culture. The wife of King Louis VII of France and later the wife of his enemy Henry of Anjou, who became king of England, she patronized some of the troubadours, whose vernacular lyrics celebrated the personal expression of emotion and a passionate declaration of service to women. Love, marriage, and the pursuit of women were also the subject of the new romance literature, which flourished in northern Europe and was the inspiration behind concepts of courtly love. However, as Swabey points out, historians in the past have misjudged Eleanor, whose independent spirit fueled their misogynist attitudes. Similarly, Eleanor's divorce and subsequent stormy marriage have colored ideas about medieval "love courts" and courtly love, interpretations of which have now been challenged by scholars. The twelfth century is set in context, with commentaries on feudalism, the tenets of Christianity, and the position of women, as well as summaries of the cultural and philosophical background, the cathedral schools and universities, the influence of Islam, the revival of classical learning, vernacular literature, and Gothic architecture. Swabey provides two biographical chapters on Eleanor and two on the emergence of the troubadours and the origin of courtly love through verse romances. Within this latter subject Swabey also details the story of Abelard and Heloise, the treatise of Andreas Capellanus (André the Chaplain) on courtly love, and Arthurian legend as a subject of courtly love.

Genghis Khan and Mongol Rule, by George Lane, identifies the rise to power of Genghis Khan and his unification of the Mongol tribes in the thirteenth century as a kind of globalization with political, cultural, economic, mercantile, and spiritual effects akin to those of modern globalization. Normally viewed as synonymous with barbarian destruction, the rise to power of Genghis Khan and the Mongol hordes is here understood as a more positive event that initiated two centuries of regeneration and creativity. Lane discusses the nature of the society of the Eurasian steppes in the twelfth and thirteenth centuries into which Genghis Khan was born; his success at reshaping the relationship between the northern pastoral and nomadic society with the southern urban, agriculturalist society; and his unification of all the Turco-Mongol tribes in 1206 before his move to conquer Tanquit Xixia, the Chin of northern China, and the lands of Islam. Conquered thereafter were the Caucasus, the Ukraine, the Crimea, Russia, Siberia, Central Asia, Afghanistan, Pakistan, and Kashmir. After his death his sons and grandsons continued, conquering Korea, Persia, Armenia, Mesopotamia, Azerbaijan, and eastern Europe—chiefly Kiev, Poland, Moravia, Silesia, and Hungary—until 1259, the end of the Mongol Empire as a unified whole. Mongol rule created a golden age in the succeeding split of the Empire into two, the Yuan dynasty of greater China and the Il-Khanate dynasty of greater Iran. Lane adds biographies of important political figures, famous names such as Marco Polo, and artists and scientists. Documents derive from universal histories, chronicles, local histories and travel accounts, official government documents, and poetry, in French, Armenian, Georgian, Chinese, Persian, Arabic, Chaghatai Turkish, Russian, and Latin.

Joan of Arc and the Hundred Years War, by Deborah Fraioli, presents the Hundred Years War between France and England in the fourteenth and fifteenth centuries within contexts whose importance has sometimes been blurred or ignored in past studies. An episode of apparently only moderate significance, a feudal lord's seizure of his vassal's land for harboring his mortal enemy, sparked the Hundred Years War, yet on the face of it the event should not have led inevitably to war. But the lord was the king of France and the vassal the king of England, who resented losing his claim to the French throne to his Valois cousin. The land in dispute, extending roughly from Bordeaux to the Pyrenees mountains, was crucial coastline for the economic interests of both kingdoms. The series of skirmishes, pitched battles, truces, stalemates, and diplomatic wrangling that resulted from the confiscation of English Aquitaine by the French form the narrative of this Anglo-French conflict, which was in fact not given the name Hundred Years War until the nineteenth century.

Fraioli emphasizes how dismissing women's inheritance and succession rights came at the high price of unleashing discontent in their male heirs, including Edward III, Robert of Artois, and Charles of Navarre. Fraioli also demonstrates the centrality of side issues, such as Flemish involvement in the war, the peasants' revolts that resulted from the costs of the war, and Joan of Arc's unusually clear understanding of French "sacred kingship." Among the primary sources provided are letters from key players such as Edward III, Etienne Marcel, and Joan of Arc; a supply list for towns about to be besieged; and a contemporary poem by the celebrated scholar and court poet Christine de Pizan in praise of Joan of Arc.

Magna Carta, by Katherine Drew, is a detailed study of the importance of the Magna Carta in comprehending England's legal and constitutional history. Providing a model for the rights of citizens found in the United States Declaration of Independence and Constitution's first ten amendments, the Magna Carta has had a role in the legal and parliamentary history of all modern states bearing some colonial or government connection with the British Empire. Constructed at a time when modern nations began to appear, in the early thirteenth century, the Magna Carta (signed in 1215) presented a formula for balancing the liberties of the people with the power of modern governmental institutions. This unique English document influenced the growth of a form of law (the English common law) and provided a vehicle for the evolution of representative (parliamentary) government. Drew demonstrates how the Magna Carta came to be—the roles of the Church, the English towns, barons, common law, and the parliament in its making—as well as how myths concerning its provisions were established. Also provided are biographies of Thomas Becket, Charlemagne, Frederick II, Henry II and his sons, Innocent III, and many other key figures, and primary documents—among them, the Magna Cartas of 1215 and 1225, and the Coronation Oath of Henry I.

Medieval Castles, by Marilyn Stokstad, traces the historical, political, and social function of the castle from the late eleventh century to the sixteenth by means of a typology of castles. This typology ranges from the early "motte and bailey"—military fortification, and government and economic center—to the palace as an expression of the castle owners' needs and purposes. An introduction defines the various contexts—military, political, economic, and social—in which the castle appeared in the Middle Ages. A concluding interpretive essay suggests the impact of the castle and its symbolic role as an idealized construct lasting until the modern day.

Medieval Cathedrals, by William Clark, examines one of the chief contributions of the Middle Ages, at least from an elitist perspective—that is, the religious architecture found in the cathedral ("chair" of the bishop) or great church, studied in terms of its architecture, sculpture, and stained glass. Clark begins with a brief contextual history of the concept of the bishop and his role within the church hierarchy, the growth of the church in the early Christian era and its affiliation with the bishop (deriving from that of the bishop of Rome), and the social history of cathedrals. Because of economic and political conflicts among the three authorities who held power in medieval towns—the king, the bishop, and the cathedral clergy—cathedral construction and maintenance always remained a vexed issue, even though the owners—the cathedral clergy—usually held the civic responsibility for the cathedral. In an interpretive essay, Clark then focuses on Reims Cathedral in France, because both it and the bishop's palace survive, as well as on contemporary information about surrounding buildings. Clark also supplies a historical overview on the social, political, and religious history of the cathedral in the Middle Ages: an essay on patrons, builders, and artists; aspects of cathedral construction (which was not always successful); and then a chapter on Romanesque and Gothic cathedrals and a "gazetteer" of twenty-five important examples.

The Medieval City, by Norman J. G. Pounds, documents the origin of the medieval city in the flight from the dangers or difficulties found in the country, whether economic, physically threatening, or cultural. Identifying the attraction of the city in its urbanitas, its "urbanity," or the way of living in a city, Pounds discusses first its origins in prehistoric and classical Greek urban revolutions. During the Middle Ages, the city grew primarily between the eleventh and thirteenth centuries, remaining essentially the same until the Industrial Revolution. Pounds provides chapters on the medieval city's planning, in terms of streets and structures; life in the medieval city; the roles of the Church and the city government in its operation; the development of crafts and trade in the city; and the issues of urban health, wealth, and welfare. Concluding with the role of the city in history, Pounds suggests that the value of the city depended upon its balance of social classes, its need for trade and profit to satisfy personal desires through the accumulation of wealth and its consequent economic power, its political power as a representative body within the kingdom, and its social role in the rise of literacy and education and in nationalism. Indeed, the concept of a middle class, a bourgeoisie, derives from the city—from the bourg, or "borough." According to Pounds, the rise of modern civilization would not have taken place without the growth of the city in the Middle Ages and its concomitant artistic and cultural contribution.

Medieval Science and Technology, by Elspeth Whitney, examines science and technology from the early Middle Ages to 1500 within the context of the classical learning that so influenced it. She looks at institutional history, both early and late, and what was taught in the medieval schools and, later, the universities (both of which were overseen by the Catholic Church). Her discussion of Aristotelian natural philosophy illustrates its impact on the medieval scientific worldview. She presents chapters on the exact sciences, meaning mathematics, astronomy, cosmology, astrology, statics, kinematics, dynamics, and optics; the biological and earth sciences, meaning chemistry and alchemy, medicine, zoology, botany, geology and meteorology, and geography; and technology. In an interpretive conclusion, Whitney demonstrates the impact of medieval science on the preconditions and structure that permitted the emergence of the modern world. Most especially, technology transformed an agricultural society into a more commercial and engine-driven society: waterpower and inventions like the blast furnace and horizontal loom turned iron working and cloth making into manufacturing operations. The invention of the mechanical clock helped to organize human activities through timetables rather than through experiential perception and thus facilitated the advent of modern life. Also influential in the establishment of a middle class were the inventions of the musket and pistol and the printing press. Technology, according to Whitney, helped advance the habits of mechanization and precise methodology. Her biographies introduce major medieval Latin and Arabic and classical natural philosophers and scientists. Extracts from various kinds of scientific treatises allow a window into the medieval concept of knowledge.

The Puebloan Society of Chaco Canyon, by Paul Reed, is unlike other volumes in this series, whose historic events boast a long-established historical record. Reed's study offers instead an original reconstruction of the Puebloan Indian society of Chaco, in what is now New Mexico, but originally extending into Colorado, Utah, and Arizona. He is primarily interested in its leaders, ritual and craft specialists, and commoners during the time of its chief flourishing, in the eleventh and twelfth centuries, as understood from archaeological data alone. To this new material he adds biographies of key Euro-American archaeologists and other individuals from the nineteenth and twentieth centuries who have made important discoveries about Chaco Canyon. Also provided are documents of archaeological description and narrative from early explorers' journals and archaeological reports, narratives, and monographs. In his overview chapters, Reed discusses the cultural and environmental setting of Chaco Canyon; its history (in terms of exploration and research); the Puebloan society and how it emerged chronologically; the Chaco society and how it appeared in 1100 C.E.; the "Outliers," or outlying communities of Chaco; Chaco as a ritual center of the eleventh-century Pueblo world; and, finally, what is and is not known about Chaco society. Reed concludes that ritual and ceremony played an important role in Chacoan society and that ritual specialists, or priests, conducted ceremonies, maintained ritual artifacts, and charted the ritual calendar. Its social organization matches no known social pattern or type: it was complicated, multiethnic, centered around ritual and ceremony, and without any overtly hierarchical political system. The Chacoans were ancestors to the later Pueblo people, part of a society that rose, fell, and evolved within a very short time period.

The Rise of Islam, by Matthew Gordon, introduces the early history of the Islamic world, beginning in the late sixth century with the career of the Prophet Muhammad (c. 570–c. 632) on the Arabian Peninsula. From Muhammad's birth in an environment of religious plurality—Christianity, Judaism, and Zoroastrianism, along with paganism, were joined by Islam—to the collapse of the Islamic empire in the early tenth century, Gordon traces the history of the Islamic community. The book covers topics that include the life of the Prophet and divine revelation (the Qur'an) to the formation of the Islamic state, urbanization in the Islamic Near East, and the extraordinary culture of Islamic letters and scholarship. In addition to a historical overview, Gordon examines the Caliphate and early Islamic Empire, urban society and economy, and the emergence, under the Abbasid Caliphs, of a "world religious tradition" up to the year 925 C.E.

As editor of this series I am grateful to have had the help of Benjamin Burford, an undergraduate Century Scholar at Rice University assigned to me in 2002–2004 for this project; Gina Weaver, a third-year graduate student in English; and Cynthia Duffy, a second-year graduate student in English, who assisted me in target-reading select chapters from some of these books in an attempt to define an audience. For this purpose I would also like to thank Gale Stokes, former dean of humanities at Rice University, for the 2003 summer research grant and portions of the 2003–2004 annual research grant from Rice University that served that end.

This series, in its mixture of traditional and new approaches to medieval history and cultures, will ensure opportunities for dialogue in the classroom in its offerings of twelve different "libraries in books." It should also propel discussion among graduate students and scholars by means of the gentle insistence throughout on the text as primal. Most especially, it invites response and further study. Given its mixture of East and West, North and South, the series symbolizes the necessity for global understanding, both of the Middle Ages and in the postmodern age.

Jane Chance, Series Editor
Houston, Texas
February 19, 2004

PREFACE

The castle was far more than a walled and turreted fortress; it was an instrument of social control and the symbol of power, authority, and wealth. This book, *Medieval Castles*, combines interpretive essays and original documents in English translation in order to examine the role of the castle in society as well as its use in war. We begin with an overview of the military and social systems operating in the Middle Ages, and we place castles and other fortified places into an appropriate context. Four chapters examine different aspects of the castle. Chapter 1, "The Great Tower," describes the early "motte and bailey" castles and the development of masonry towers and walls in the eleventh and twelfth centuries. Chapter 2, "The Castle as Fortress," considers the military aspects of castles, including siege warfare and the architectural response to attack and defense, in the twelfth and thirteenth centuries. Chapter 3, "The Castle as Headquarters," explores castles and citadels as local and regional government and economic centers in the thirteenth and fourteenth centuries. Chapter 4, "The Castle as Symbol and Palace," looks at the symbolic role of architecture and at castles as elite residences and settings for public display. A concluding interpretive chapter looks at the impact of gunpowder on castles as well as our continuing fascination with the castle as a romantic fantasy of an idealized world. Each chapter also describes specific castles and explores the ways in which they met the needs and expectations of their owners.

A selection of original documents in English translation affords the reader a chance to see castles from the point of view of the people who lived in and near them. Since references to castles in primary documents are usually brief, sometimes no more than a name and place, I have in-

cluded many short passages. I have organized the documents themati-
cally: early references and descriptions, construction, sieges, tales of trickery, daring escapes, the action of heroic men and women, life in and
outside the castle, and a few rare descriptions of the life of ordinary people. In selecting authors who are good story tellers and who give us lively
accounts of the world, I have focused on castles in today's British Isles
and France. A separate volume in this series on the Crusades includes
other regions. Brief biographies are provided for men and women men-
tioned in the text—owners and builders of the castles, and the writers
whose works provide us with information and insight into this fascinating period.

The book concludes with a glossary and bibliography. The glossary includes specialized terms used in the discussion of castle architecture. The
bibliography contains only recent books in English, in consideration of
the needs of today's students and the holdings of high school and public
libraries. The many books on castles written in the nineteenth and early
twentieth centuries and books in foreign languages are not included.

Finally, the illustrations need a brief explanation. By their very nature
castles had a short life. Their owners and builders expected them to be
attacked, their walls to be leveled, their towers to be battered down, their
courtyard buildings to be wrecked and burned. Castles standing today either have been rebuilt to satisfy the fancy of modern owners or have been
left as romantic ruins. Consequently we cannot see these buildings as
they once existed and were meant to be seen. To illustrate this book, I
have included early photographs of a few castles from the Gramstorff Collection, Photographic Archive, National Gallery of Art, Washington,
DC; my own photographs; and photographs taken by my sister and niece,
some as recently as 2004. The Gramstorff photographs show the castles
before modern restoration and rebuilding and without the parking lots,
shopping centers, and amusement parks which so often surround historic
monuments in the twenty-first century. The Stokstad-Leider photographs
give an idea of what one may expect to see today. Yes, we have tried to
screen out the modern world, but we must ask our readers to approach
their castle studies with open minds and active imaginations.

I would like to thank librarians Susan Craig, Richard Clement, Sarah
Goodwin-Thiel, and Richard Ring of the University of Kansas, photo
archivists Ruth Philbrick and Andrea Gibbs of the National Gallery,
Washington, DC, my research assistant Reed Anderson, high school con-

sultant Christina Clement, and those who have been patient with me, Karen and Anna Leider, Katherine Giele, Anta Montet White, Katherine Stannard, and Nancy Dinneen. A special thanks to Keith Dawson, who recaptured the pieces of text floating in cyberspace, the staff of the Spencer Research Library and the Murphy Library of Art and Architecture at the University of Kansas, and especially to series editor Jane Chance and Greenwood editor Michael Hermann.

CHRONOLOGY

1050: THE MOTTE AND BAILEY CASTLE

1035	William the Bastard becomes duke of Normandy.
1054	Separation of Roman (Catholic) and Byzantine (Orthodox) churches becomes final.
1060–1108	Philip I rules in France.
1066–71/72	Normans conquer England, build castles.
1066–87	William the Conqueror, duke of Normandy, rules as king of England.
1066–1100	Tower of London is built.
1070s	The Hospitalers are founded.
1085	Christians capture Toledo in Spain.
1087–89	First castle of Rochester is built.
1095	Pope Urban calls for the First Crusade.
1096–99	Crusaders undertake the First Crusade.
1099	Crusaders capture Jerusalem.

1100: THE GREAT TOWER

1100–35	Henry I rules in England.
1108–37	Louis VI the Fat rules in France.

1118	Order of Knights Templar is founded.
1120s	Rochester and Kenilworth castles are built.
1136–54	English civil wars are fought.
1137–80	Louis VII rules in France.
1137–52	Eleanor of Aquitaine is queen of France.
1146	St. Bernard preaches the Second Crusade.
1146/47–49	Second Crusade is undertaken.
1152–90	Frederick Barbarossa reigns as Holy Roman Emperor.
1154–89	Henry II Plantagenet rules in England; Eleanor of Aquitaine marries Henry and becomes queen of England.
1160	Tomar, Portugal, is built.
1165–1200	Cathedral of Notre Dame, Paris, is constructed; nave is built 1180–1200.
1170	Thomas à Becket is murdered.
1173	Becket is canonized.
1174	Henry II does penance.
1174–93	Saladin leads the Muslims.
1180–1223	Philip Augustus rules in France.
1180s–90s	Tower at Kenilworth is built.
1187	The Muslims led by Saladin capture Jerusalem.
1189–99	Richard the Lion Hearted rules in England.
1189–1204	Eleanor of Aquitaine is queen mother of England.
1190–93	Third Crusade is undertaken.
1196–98	King Richard builds Chateau Gaillard.

1200: THE ENCEINTE OR ENCLOSURE CASTLE; FORTIFIED MANOR HOUSES AND CITIES

1202–4	Fourth Crusade is undertaken.
1203–4	The French capture Chateau Gaillard.
1204	Western crusaders capture Constantinople.
1204–61	Constantinople becomes a Latin kingdom.
1205	The French capture the castle of Chinon.
1215	King John signs the Magna Carta.
1216	Rochester is besieged.
1216–72	Henry III rules in England.
1226–34	Blanche of Castile is queen mother and regent for Louis IX.
1226–70	Louis IX (St. Louis) rules in France.
1228–38	Castle of Angers is built.
1248–54	Louis IX leads the Seventh Crusade; he establishes Aigues Mortes as a port.
1267–70	Louis IX undertakes a crusade to Tunis.
1272–1307	Edward I rules in England.
1278–1309	Master James of St. George designs castles in Wales.
1285–90	Harlech Castle is built.
1285–1314	Philip IV, the Fair, rules in France.
1285–1322	Caernarfon town and castle are built.
1290	License is issued to crenellate Stokesay.
1291	Muslims drive Christians from Holy Land.
1297	Louis IX is canonized.

1300: CITADELS AND ROYAL CITIES; THE RESIDENTIAL CASTLES; MANOR HOUSES

1305–78	The Pope lives in Avignon.
1307–14	Templars are persecuted.
1307–27	Edward II rules in England.
1319	King Dinis of Portugal founds the Order of Christ.
1321	Dante dies.
1326–27	The Toll castles, Gutenfels and Pfaltz, are built in Germany.
1327–77	Edward III rules in England.
1328–47	Bishop Henry Gower, St. David's, Wales, builds the Bishop's Palace.
1337–1453	France and England engage in the Hundred Years War.
1340–99	John of Gaunt is duke of Lancaster.
August 26, 1346	Gunpowder is used in Battle of Crecy.
1347–48	Black Death begins.
1350–64	John II, the Good, rules in France.
1364–80	Charles V rules in France.
1370–82	The Bastille in Paris is built.
1372–88	John of Gaunt claims the kingdom of Castile.
1377–99	Richard II rules in England.
1378–1417	Schism occurs in the Church; rival popes rule from Rome and Avignon.
1380–1422	Charles VI rules in France.
1384	Angers Castle is rebuilt.

1386–90	Bodiam Castle is built.
1399–1413	Henry IV rules in England.

1400: THE PALATIAL CASTLE; FORTRESSES TO WITHSTAND CANNON

1400	Geoffrey Chaucer dies.
1413–22	Henry V, king of England, defeats French at Agincourt, marries Katherine of France (after death of Henry, Katherine marries Owen Tudor).
1415	Pleasance at Kenilworth is built.
1418–60	Henry the Navigator finances expeditions in the Atlantic and along the African coast.
1422–61	Charles VII rules in France.
1422–71	Henry VI rules in England.
1427–50	Charles VII lives at Chinon.
1431	Joan of Arc is burned at the stake in Rouen.
1432	Rogier van der Weyden paints *St. George and the Dragon*.
1453	Constantinople falls to the Turks.
1454	Johannes Gutenberg uses moveable type in a printing press.
1455–85	Wars of the Roses is fought in England.
1483–85	Richard III rules in England.
1485–1509	Henry (Tudor) VII rules in England.
1487	Portuguese explorers sail around the Cape of Good Hope, Africa.
1492	Columbus reaches America.
1492	Granada, the last Moorish kingdom in Spain, falls to the Christians.

1500: THE PALACE

1509–47	Henry VIII rules in England.
1513–21	Castle (Chateau) of Chenonceau is built.
1558–1603	Elizabeth I rules in England.
1575	Elizabeth visits Kenilworth as guest of Robert Dudley, Earl of Leicester.
1575	Mary Queen of Scots visits Chenonceau.

OVERVIEW: CASTLES IN CONTEXT

ROMANCE OR REALITY?

The idea of a castle inspires us to dream of magical places far away and long ago. We owe our romantic image of the Middle Ages to the fantasies of authors like Sir Thomas Malory (c. 1416–71) in the fifteenth century, Edmund Spenser (1532–99) in the sixteenth century, or Alfred, Lord Tennyson (1809–92) in the nineteenth century. They wrote about wonderful characters like King Arthur and the Knights of the Round Table, Queen Guenevere and Sir Lancelot, Morgan le Fay, and fairy queens and swan maidens. Through their eyes we see heroic knights battling demons, magicians, witches, and dragons. Their warriors are not young thugs, trained killers who were destined to die of festering wounds. These knights of romance are handsome youths dedicated to truth and goodness and the defense of virtue as personified by beautiful damsels in distress.

Transformed by gleaming armor, his miraculous sword in hand, the gallant knight rides through the deep dark forest mounted on his mighty white steed, ready to face down every imaginable peril—dragons, serpents, or, best of all, an evil knight in polished black armor ready to fight to the death. Triumphant, our hero frees the impotent aged king and helpless queen, who in gratitude give him their only daughter as his bride and at least half the kingdom as his reward.

Heroic themes of yesteryear still resonate in popular culture: Robin Hood confronting the sheriff of Nottingham; the Lone Ranger, astride his horse Silver, bringing justice to the Wild West; and Sir Gawain facing the perils of the forest and an enchanted castle. We even have our own contemporary "knights in shining armor," for example, the football quarterback, masked by protective "armor" decorated with heraldic colors and symbolic emblems and animals, who leads his team of loyal companions against an oncoming horde intent on breaking through his defenses while preventing him from taking over their home territory.

Our hero eventually needs more than a warhorse, faithful squire, and shining armor. He must have a base of operations—a castle. Castles pepper the medieval landscape—the knight's own stronghold, his lord's castle, and the castles of friends and enemies. Naturally the castles of romance are no ordinary fortresses, but architectural fantasies with a jumble of walls, towers, and fortified gates rising on the crest of a hill or clinging to a cliff overlooking a swiftly flowing river. A moat and drawbridge block the approach to the castle. Massive doors and the sliding grill of a portcullis defend its entrance while flanking towers provide surveillance points, and their vaults hide murder holes.

St. George and the Dragon

The fifteenth-century Flemish painter Rogier van der Weyden created just such a castle, rising above a prosperous fortified port city and surrounding countryside, as a background for his painting of *St. George and the Dragon* (see Figure 1). In the painting the warrior saint, in glistening armor and impossibly long elegant sleeves, drives his lance through the neck of a hapless dragon and so saves yet another princess. The princess kneels in the grass, careful not to muss her carefully arranged brocade gown. She modestly casts her eyes downward, confident in her champion's victory, while in the background, the residents of the prosperous port city go about their business, unaware of the drama taking place outside their city walls. Travelers approach the city gates, and an innkeeper hangs out a welcome sign. Round towers reinforce the city walls, and on the heights of a strange, dream-like mountain, a castle's towers and walls, spires and roofs soar upward. For all his meticulous realism in depicting the details of city buildings and surrounding countryside, Rogier has created a castle as fantastic as the dragon. Although the castle's crenellated walls and towers recall the military architecture of earlier centuries, the luxury of the residence now captures the artist's imagination.

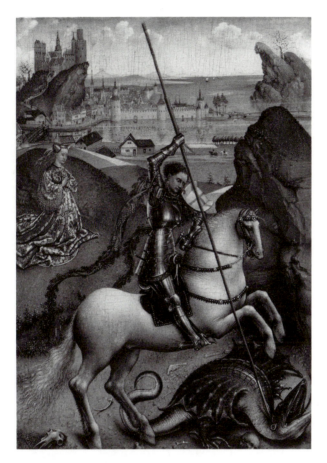

Figure 1. Rogier van der Weyden. *St. George and the Dragon.* Fantastic rock outcrops frame the scene of St. George's encounter with the dragon. In contrast Rogier records the prosperous countryside and a walled city nestled below a large castle with meticulous realism. The castle's high walls and towers protect an elegant residence and chapel. Lower city walls with strong towers surround houses and shops, large churches, and public buildings. *Rogier van der Weyden. St. George and the Dragon (c. 1432/1435). Oil on wood panel, 5 5/8 × 4 1/8 in. Ailsa Mellon Bruce Fund 1966. 1.1, Board of Trustees, National Gallery of Art, Washington, DC.*

Figure 2. Windsor Castle from the river Thames. The twelfth-century great tower rises 215 feet above the river, its upper half added in 1828–32 for King George IV. The walls and buildings have been rebuilt or heavily restored since the castle remains a royal residence. The roof, turrets, and part of the great window of St. George's chapel (begun in 1475) can be seen at the right. *Photograph by George Washington Wilson (Scottish, 1823–93). Gramstorff Collection, Photographic Archives, National Gallery of Art, Washington, DC.*

Windsor Castle

Whether in ruins or pleasantly restored, castles today can still seem just as dream-like. Windsor Castle, as seen in an early photograph by the Scottish architectural photographer George Washington Wilson, presents a romantic image beside the river Thames (see Figure 2). Windsor Castle's lofty tower and mighty walls make this stronghold a symbol of royal and feudal power. Within these walls stands the chapel of St. George, who remains patron saint of England even though the Catholic Church no longer recognizes George as a saint.

Windsor Castle is the home of the English royal family. William the Conqueror built a timber castle beside the Thames after his victory over the Anglo-Saxons in 1066. Remodeling and modernizing have continued at the castle ever since. Henry II replaced the original wood and earthen structure with stone in the twelfth century, and Henry III finished the stone walls and towers in the thirteenth century. In the next century Edward III added fine residential buildings and a chapel dedicated to St. George. Henry VIII and Elizabeth I sometimes lived in the castle, and Charles II ordered the architect Hugh May and the master sculptor Grinling Gibbons to modernize the living areas after the seventeenth-century civil war. In the eighteenth century James Wyatt and in the nineteenth century his nephew Sir Jeffry Wyatville modernized the castle yet again. They created the "Gothicized" buildings we see today. At the end of the twentieth century, a devastating fire engulfed St. George's Hall, which has now been rebuilt.

Were castles really as rough and rugged as their owners? The answer seems to be, "not necessarily." Castles were indeed rough and rugged fortresses, the product of an essentially elite, masculine warrior society, what today we call a feudal society. But they were also among the finest buildings of their times—secure, well-built residences that supported the complex rituals of noble life. To understand how castle form came to meet castle function, we must look briefly at the castle's social and economic underpinnings.

THE MEDIEVAL SOCIAL ORDER

Feudalism, a term first used in the seventeenth century (the word comes from *feudum*, a fief or grant of land), became the political and social system characteristic of western Europe during the Middle Ages. This system evolved over many centuries.

After the collapse of the Roman Empire in the fourth century, Europe experienced a breakdown of law and order and a decline in living standards. During a brief period at the end of the eighth and beginning of the ninth century the great warlord and emperor Charlemagne and his heirs established a central government, but Charlemagne's three grandsons soon broke up the empire into separate kingdoms. As the Carolingian empire gave way to internal strife and outside dangers, rival families fought for wealth and power.

Meanwhile, Vikings, Slavs, Magyars (Hungarians), and Muslims threatened western Europe. Local strongmen led bands of warriors and formed private armies. They lived in timber blockhouses and towers set behind earthworks and stockades. For a price they took farmers under their protection. What was at first a simple agreement between a military chief and the civilians who needed protection slowly evolved into a system of formal oaths and grants of land. The Celtic/Germanic warrior tradition of a lord and his people bound by oaths of loyalty and mutual support joined with the ancient Roman idea of patrons who retained their land but made grants to clients or tenant farmers. By the tenth and eleventh centuries this system of lords and vassals, known today as feudalism, replaced kingdoms and empires, and effective government lay in the hands of private individuals.

During the Middle Ages, land (not money) was the basis of wealth, power, and authority, and a very small group of men—and a few women—controlled the land. As the political and economic system evolved, especially in France and England, the king, who in theory held the land in trust for God, gave his powerful friends parcels of land to exploit in exchange for military support and assistance in administering justice. Vassals would owe service in the feudal lord's army and in his court, in exchange for food and lodging at the lord's castle. But the expense of maintaining an army and running a castle was enormous. As a result, major landholders complicated the system by subdividing and parceling out their lands to retainers under similar terms.

As a money economy began to develop, it became convenient for the vassal to pay the lord instead of performing service. This was known as "shield money" or "scutage." Eventually landholding became hereditary, with titles, duties, and resources passed on from father to children, in most cases to the oldest son.

Never as neat or well organized as many descriptions suggest, in essence feudalism involved the exchange of grants of land for military and political service, sealed by personal oaths between the lord and the vassal. The castle has been called the perfect architectural expression of the European feudal age.

The Code of Chivalry

The Church attempted to regulate this rather violent society, and eventually a code of honor evolved known as the code of chivalry. (The word *chivalry* comes from the Latin word for horse, *caballus*, as does the word *cavalry*.) Those who aspired to be knights had to have aristocratic ancestors and wealth enough to own warhorses and armor and to provide for a team of supporters. After years of training, a young man became a knight—his status as a noble, mounted warrior confirmed by a ritual that included solemn oaths and vigils. The knight swore to live by a Christian code of conduct, to honor and protect the Church, the weak and elderly, and especially women. He was expected to behave courteously, generously, and graciously. Knights displayed their athletic and military skills in tournaments, which were in effect mock battles. Favorite forms of recreation were hunting with horses, hounds, and falcons and board games like chess, which was part of the warrior's training in strategy. Eventually knights—encouraged by royal and noble ladies like Eleanor of Aquitaine—became courtiers, attendants at the royal court, well versed in the civilian arts of music, poetry, and polite conversation.

Manorialism and the Agricultural Estate

The king and nobles, the bishops and abbots, all of whom operated within the feudal system of allegiances and loyalties, depended for their wealth on an agricultural system known as manorialism. The agricultural estate, or manor, varied in size and value but usually included productive fields and orchards, pasture land, and forests. Free peasants and serfs (people who were legally free but tied to the land) provided the labor in both their own fields and those belonging to the lord of the manor (who might be an individual or an entity such as a monastery). In most places people lived in villages. At the center of the manorial village stood the lord's manor house, which might be fortified and have such necessities for a self-sufficient community as an oven, smithy, mill, and often a wine press—all of which belonged to the lord of the manor, and which the villagers paid to use. Since agricultural surpluses might be slim, nobles often held several manors and moved from manor to manor in order to oversee the estates, administer justice, and collect rents and taxes paid in goods. Brigandage was rampant, and the farmers also suffered from the destruction of their crops during wartime. Like the feudal system, manorialism reflected the unstable conditions of the early Middle Ages. Class distinctions created what is known today as a stratified society, with the clergy and the warrior/administrators at the top and the workers—peasants and serfs—at the bottom.

The Place of the Church

The Church played a dominant role in the Middle Ages, and the clergy stood at the top of the social order. Through its rites the Church presided over all the important events in people's lives and determined their fate in the afterlife, in heaven or hell. Wealthy people gave land and treasure to the Church as thank offerings and in hopes of influencing their chances of salvation. With ample resources, bishops and abbots commanded the best talent and materials to build for the glory of God. Architecturally, church buildings led the way in the sophistication of their designs and building techniques and the splendor of their decoration. Every parish had its church and most noble families had their private chapels. Daily services and prayers, the celebration of the festivals of the Church, the invocation of saints in times of difficulty, the rituals of knighthood and the courts all meant that a castle needed a chapel, even when a parish church stood in a nearby village. The chapel might be a separate building located within the castle walls, but it might also be incorporated into the gatehouse or the great tower. A large castle might have both a private chapel for the family and a church for the parish.

The Role of Women

Women played a greater role than might be expected in this elite warrior society, as heiresses and chatelaines in charge of castles (see Documents 44–53). Since land was the basis of status and power, estates were kept intact by being passed on to the oldest son rather than being divided among all the children. In spite of high infant mortality and short life expectancies, a family hoped that at least one son survived to inherit lands and titles. Younger sons hoped to gain an estate of their own by marrying an heiress. Consequently a young noblewoman (or later the daughter of a prosperous merchant or peasant) might become a pawn in the marriage game, if she brought land and treasure into a family as her dowry. Of course, a few younger sons and daughters gained positions in the court or the Church through their extraordinary personal skills.

A strong and clever woman acted for her husband when he was serving his feudal lord in court or at war, and she might command the defense of the castle or fortified manor house in his absences. Even in peacetime, her responsibilities were heavy. She managed a large, self-sufficient household, sometimes composed of hundreds of individuals, which moved regularly from one manor to another. She oversaw the care and education of children as well as the health and well-being of the community. In an age when the only effective medicine came from the herb garden, she was gardener and herbalist. She also provided for the cultural life in the castle through music and dancing, pageants and oral poetry.

If a woman's husband died before a son came of age, she tried to maintain control of the property against the encroachment of greedy uncles and overlords. As a widow she kept part of her dowry.

An alternate career path for a woman lay in the Church, where as a nun she escaped the dangers of childbirth. In the convent she could hold any position except that of priest, and as an abbess or prioress she had great power and responsibility.

The Rise of the Merchant Class

Although Europe remained largely rural during the Middle Ages, people gradually moved from the agricultural estates to towns where they became merchants and artisans. While some cities had survived in a reduced state since the days of urbanized Rome, others grew up or were founded at strategic crossroads, at fords in rivers, or around a village market, often beside protective castle walls. Rogier painted just such a large prosperous city as a background to *St. George and the Dragon* (see Figure 1). City people, the burghers (*burh* or *burg* was a Germanic word for city), for all their entrepreneurial skills, held their fortunes in goods and money, that is, moveable property, not land, and so they remained outside the traditional social and economic (feudal-manorial) system. As trade and commerce revived and an economy based on money emerged, their power and social standing grew.

Kings who recognized the importance of money as a means to hire their own soldiers and free themselves from overly powerful vassals began to ally themselves with the burghers. They established new towns where they granted special privileges and collected taxes. Nevertheless, the medieval social order continued to place the clergy in the highest rank, followed by the landed nobility, and at the bottom everyone else, whether they were wealthy merchants and artisans in the towns or farmers on the land.

In this complex and shifting but highly stratified society, material symbols—especially a crowd of liveried retainers performing their duties in an imposing castle—became a very important way for a noble to show his importance. Livery (distinctive dress) identified the members of a noble household by means of the design of garments, the colors of cloth, the embroidered symbols, and even metal badges (Document 66). Meanwhile the castle building itself provided a setting for the rituals of daily life. The castle stood as an outward sign of aristocratic authority, wealth, power, and privilege. Ultimately the height of castle walls and towers became as important for their symbolic value as for their defensive capability. The castle as an architectural form changed to reflect and accommodate changing needs, functions, and expectations. When explosives came into use in the fourteenth century, making walls easy targets, the massive towers of the twelfth century gave way to the complex and decorative turrets we see in Rogier's painting of St. George.

WHAT IS A CASTLE?

Before we continue our story we must stop to ask, "What is a castle?" Once a castle was defined simply as the fortified and self-sufficient dwelling of an individual feudal lord. Today we know that castles had many functions, both practical and symbolic. The castle was a new architectural form—part fortress, part residence, part statehouse, part theatrical stage. Furthermore, every castle was different, depending on the wealth of the builder, the reason for the castle (control of territory, border, coastlines), the local geography (availability of naturally defensible sites), the knowledge of the master builder or patron, the available materials, the degree of urgency (speed), and finally the building traditions of the region (the techniques the workmen knew and used). In short, there is no such thing as a typical castle; a castle was a very special building whose form and function answered the needs of people living in Europe from the eleventh through the fifteenth century.

Word Origins

Where does the word *castle* come from? Strangely enough, medieval writers never made up a new word to describe this new building type. They continued to use Latin words like *castrum* (pl. *castra*) and *castellum* (*castella*), meaning a town, a walled enclosure, a stronghold, or sometimes simply a tower. Ancient Romans called any stronghold or walled place a *castrum*, and used the diminutive form, *castellum*, for everything from a fortress to a dwelling on a hill. Ancient Roman military camps with ditches and palisades, for example, were also called *castra*. In the early Middle Ages, authors used these words for any inhabited place. But meanings changed, and from a rather vague designation for any walled enclosure, "castle" came to mean a specific kind of building. By the eleventh century *castellum* had entered the vernacular languages of Europe as castle (English), castillo (Spanish), castello (Italian), or chateau (French), although burh, burg, borg, berg, or burgh remained the preferred form in Germanic languages.

As we use the word today, a castle is not a palace, which is unfortified, although a castle and a palace are both imposing residences. Nor is it a fort, for that word implies a purely military function and a garrison. Neither is a castle a walled city, although a royal castle may house as many people as a town, for the castle—even with all its buildings and inhabitants—has a single owner. In short, a castle combines a variety of building types in a new way, often using the same kind of sophisticated decoration and fine masonry to be found in religious architecture. A castle was a secure place to live and to administer the surrounding estate, and as a headquarters and court of justice, it became the visible symbol of its owner's authority.

Castle Remains Today

Castle building and constant castle repair—like any war effort—ate up the resources of the land, both in materials and labor (see Documents 15–19). The very nature of the castle almost guarantees that it shall be destroyed—either in war or by official decree. Siege warfare required the breaching of castle walls and the destruction of towers. As rulers brought feudal holdings under a central government, they could not afford to have castles in the hands of possible rivals or unruly subjects. A castle is said to be "slighted" when it is officially destroyed. Over time, nature also adds to the castle's disintegration, recapturing its own with vines and underbrush and even trees. To visit a castle is to see broken walls, roofless halls, and sometimes only stone foundations and earthworks. When a castle seems at first glance to be intact, we can be certain it has been rebuilt. We must turn to archeology, to historical archives, and to art history for information. Even then we need an active imagination to study castles.

EARLY FORTIFICATIONS AND DEFENSIVE STRUCTURES

Since earliest times people have built walls to protect themselves and their belongings—walls around country estates controlled livestock and protected the animals from marauding wolves or poachers. With equal determination their enemies and rivals have tried to break through those walls to kill and steal.

When a strong central authority protects borders and reduces internal crime, people have little need for fortified dwellings, although the rulers may build walls and towers to define legitimate residents and defend the country against external threats. When central authority breaks down, however, individuals are more likely to fortify their homes. The presence of castles in the landscape indicates a decline in stability and peace.

Earth and Timber Structures

As we shall see in Chapter 1, two building traditions existed side by side—the earth and timber structures of northern and western Europe and the masonry buildings of the Roman Empire and the Mediterranean world. Surrounded by great forests, the Celtic people in northern and western Europe turned to timber and earth for building materials. They lived in villages of timber and turf houses surrounded by ditches, embankments (earth removed for the ditch was piled beside it to make a bank), and wattle (woven branches) fences. Wherever possible they chose defensible sites. For example, the Celts in France (known as Gauls) built their villages on hilltops with commanding views and difficult access, while in Ireland they built on islands in lakes or swamps. They strengthened the sites with timber palisades and towers and complex earthworks including ditches filled with spiked poles. On a relatively secure site they might use only wattle fences that formed corrals rather than effective defensive works. These cities and forts usually had a circular plan, since a circular wall encloses the most land within the shortest wall. When the Gauls confronted Caesar (58–49 B.C.E.), they retreated behind the massive earth and timber walls of the hilltop oppidum, Alesia. The Romans then laid siege and defeated them by using complex siege engines such as battering rams and catapults.

Motte and Bailey

In western Europe in the ninth century, the breakup of the Carolingian empire made the need for personal protection and fortified homes necessary again. The amount and intensity of local warfare increased, and later the attacks of the Vikings from the north and the Magyars from the east made the defense of borders mandatory. In the ninth century the Norse Vikings, masters of the hit-and-run offense, dedicated their skills to ship building and erected relatively light fortifications. They built circular base camps and trading centers that became true cities. When in the tenth and eleventh centuries these Northmen settled in northern France and began to fortify their holdings, they continued to build in earth and timber. They developed the motte and bailey castle, a form popular with the Germanic peoples all over Europe but most often associated today with the Normans.

Stone and Mortar

Into this land of earth and timber architecture the Romans introduced stone and mortar. Heirs of a long tradition of masonry building in the Mediterranean world, the Romans perfected the use of materials and techniques such as rubble and concrete, bricks and mortar, and arches and vaults. Masters of efficient organization, they laid out rectangular army camps and cities with major crossing streets and regularly disposed houses or barracks.

Hadrian's Wall

Hadrian's Wall (built about 122–25), which runs across northern England, is typical of the Roman frontier defenses. A single masonry wall with a concrete core and stone facings, the wall was seventy-three miles long, between seven feet, six inches and nine feet, six inches thick, and probably about fifteen feet high. In some places extensive earthworks also survive. The wall follows the crest of hills, and it presented a sufficient obstacle to encroachment by native people. Punctuated by towers at mile intervals (popularly known as "mile castles"), the wall functioned as a boundary and lookout post as well as a defense. Men walking or standing on the top of the wall were protected by crenellations—raised masonry panels (merlons) alternating with low sections (crenels) over which soldiers could observe the wall or shoot at invaders. The wall's height and thickness provided protection against direct attack, but limited sight lines from the wall-walk made any wall difficult to defend.

Sixteen forts housed the soldiers who patrolled the wall. Gates consisted of a pair of doors flanked either by semiround (D-shaped) or square towers. Such a wall was usually deemed to be sufficient protection. The Aurelian wall around the city of Rome itself was a single wall and was only strengthened in later years when the empire went into a decline.

Theodosian Walls

The last great defensive work of the ancient world—and the first of the medieval age—was built to protect the city of Constantinople. The new Rome has been known by many names—Byzantion (the original Greek port), Constantinople (Constantine's city), or later Byzantium, and today Istanbul. For his new capital city, Constantine selected a small Greek port, Byzantion, on a peninsula. The sea and a sea wall protected most of the city, but the land side of the peninsula required a heavier defensive system. When the emperor Theodosius expanded the city early in the fifth century, he ordered double walls and a moat for the vulnerable side. The Theodosian walls stood as a model for medieval builders. So effective were the walls that they protected the city until 1453 when the Turks blasted through them using cannon.

Byzantine success depended on a system that combined vertical defense with defense in depth, that is, high walls and towers with double walls and a moat. The walls were built of stone and concrete and bonded with layers of brick, creating a colorful banded effect. The great inner wall was fifteen feet, six inches thick and had ninety-six towers, each of which could become an independent fortress. No one was allowed to build next to the wall; consequently, no traitor could bore through the walls from the back of his house. The open space also permitted rapid deployment of troops along the wall. Beyond the great wall, Theodosius' engineers constructed a lower second wall about six feet, six inches thick; men on the high inner wall could see and shoot over the heads of those on the lower outer wall. A moat (water-filled ditch) defended the outer wall from anyone attempting to tunnel under it or batter it down. The moat was deep and wide and reinforced by low walls.

Figure 3. Pembroke Castle, Wales. Pembroke Castle was a major Norman stronghold in Wales and the base of operations of Richard FitzGilbert, known as "Strongbow," during the Norman conquest of Ireland. After Strongbow's death, his daughter married the famous warrior William Marshall. The earl and countess lived at Pembroke, creating the finest castle in southern Wales. *Photograph: Karen Leider.*

To review: an attacking army faced a triple line of defense. If they were able to bridge the moat, they had to break through a wall, only to be trapped in front of an even stronger wall overlooked by fortress-towers. Such elaborate defenses required the vast resources of an empire to build. No western prince could afford the materials and the crew of skilled masons necessary to replicate the walls of Constantinople. Not until the twelfth century did such complex defensive structures appear in the West.

THE ROLE OF THE MEDIEVAL CASTLE

The medieval castle's role was to provide a secure aristocratic residence and a military headquarters (Figures 3 and 4). A castle enabled the resident commander to control the surrounding territory including border and key transportation hubs. Located in a defensible position, the castle provided a center from which the lord (or his castellan or constable) oversaw his manors and where he fulfilled his feudal obligation to administer justice (for this reason the castle often included both a great hall

Figure 4. Great tower, Pembroke Castle, Wales. William Marshall built the great tower about 1200 in the most up-to-date style. Round towers entirely of masonry with double fighting galleries had proved to be more effective than the old square towers. The vast open space within the castle walls would have been filled with wood and thatch shelters for people and animals. The foundations and some walls of masonry buildings can also be seen near the great tower. *Photograph: Karen Leider.*

and a prison). One writes and speaks of the feudal lord, and so the times dictated, but in fact the lord was often absent, and his wife or a constable took over the daily responsibility of running the castle, even on occasion defending it during an attack. The castle was a symbol of authority and the high social status of the family that owned it.

Today castle studies have concentrated on individual monuments and on the social and symbolic role of the castle, while a hundred—and even fifty—years ago scholars emphasized the castle's military aspects and the effect of the opposing forces of attack and defense in the architectural design. These roles, however, cannot be studied in isolation. For a full understanding of the medieval castle, we must examine the castle as fortress, statehouse, and residence.

The Castle and Siege Warfare

To defend themselves, local leaders revived and improved ancient techniques of fortification and assault. The castle builders (military en-

gineers) and commanders of the Middle Ages continued the siege warfare techniques developed by the Romans, modifying designs and equipment to accommodate local traditions, geography, and materials. Every
increase in offensive power was met with greater strength or cleverness
by defenders.

Chapter 2 looks at the castle as a fortification. Medieval warfare consisted of long sieges around a castle or town and relatively short battles
in the field, rarely involving a large army of more than 20,000 men. The
castle held the defensive position, and a well-built stronghold could be
taken only through extended siege. In many ways, the advantage lay with
the castle dwellers because the castle could be well provisioned and
staffed while the assembled feudal army had to live off the land. In the
hey-day of castle building, early armies consisted of a relatively undisciplined force of men who were only required to serve a limited time, usually forty days a year. Such men might be more interested in returning
to their own homes than they were in pursuing their lord's cause and
maintaining a siege.

Having decided to invest (lay siege to) the castle, the aggressor's strategy would be to block off supplies and reinforcements, and then to attempt to take the castle by force, only when negotiation, treachery, or
blockade and starvation failed. An assault on the castle was a slow affair
because the attackers had to go over, through, or under the walls and
then engage in hand-to-hand combat. To go over the wall involved the
use of scaling ladders or a mobile wooden tower called a belfry. When
moved into place, this tower allowed knights to climb the ramparts to
the wall-walk and then engage their equals in combat. A slower, but often
more effective, assault involved tunneling under the wall, causing it to
collapse. Finally, to breach the walls the attackers used battering rams
and stone-throwing machines, which were essentially very large catapults
(see Figure 14). The most powerful engine was the trebuchet (a giant
sling), which could throw huge stones with great force. None of these
siege engines have survived, but a team of twenty-first-century "re-enacters" has built and tested the trebuchet and other engines with spectacular results.

The mightiest castles of the eleventh and twelfth centuries were once
veritable war machines, although even a well-built castle could be taken
after a long siege by starvation or treachery. Castle walls and towers were
defensive structures to be smashed by ever-increasing firepower. For all

their imposing appearance, many castles stood for only a few years before they were destroyed and left in ruins. From the tenth through thirteenth centuries, castles functioned as military machines, but in the fourteenth and fifteenth centuries their role changed almost completely, and they were replaced by forts designed for artillery.

The Castle as Political and Economic Headquarters

Castles served as government centers as well as fortresses. Walls and towers provided the necessary security especially when a ruler attempted to control rebellious subjects. Within the walls, however, were increasingly splendid residences, especially a great hall where the ruler or local lord sat in state to administer justice and hear petitions. Towers served as strong rooms to protect treasure and documents. Increasing reliance on money and laws required a treasury and legal archives for records and charters. Whereas once the scribes worked in monastic scriptoria, now they labored in chancery halls. Not only the king but also his great vassals and their vassals in turn, right down to the local officials, needed imposing and secure headquarters. Chapter 3 explores the castle's political and economic role.

The Castle as Symbol: From Fortress to Palace

The first European castles were massive single towers surrounded by walls. These towers contained one or two rooms on each floor and included a basement storage area, a great hall, living rooms, and a chapel. The great hall, a single large common room, provided space where everyone lived and ate and slept. At one end on a raised platform was the lord's chair and table. Others sat and ate at portable trestle tables and benches perpendicular to the high table. These simple arrangements formed the basis of later developments, and continue today in our own tradition of a "head table" at a banquet. Window embrasures in the thick walls offered small semiprivate spaces. The service areas were located in a courtyard called the bailey. Eventually more private chambers were added and then whole suites of rooms.

Castles had always provided hospitality, but by the fourteenth and fifteenth centuries they required stables for horses, suites of rooms for guests and travelers, and apartments for retainers who expected to be housed when they were called on to serve the lord. These apartments became small versions of the lord's chambers. Castles also had to house men-at-arms and servants (who formed their own hierarchies). In short, the arrangements within the castle walls became increasingly complex and "stratified," reflecting the society at large.

Chapter 4 looks more closely at how social and symbolic needs took precedence in the late Middle Ages. The great hall, the center of daily life in earlier periods, remained the ceremonial center of the castle. There the lord received guests or supplicants and there he administered justice, gave orders, and offered hospitality. The architecture provided a setting for all this activity. To continue and even enhance the effectiveness of the lord's position, the design of portals, passages, and waiting rooms carefully controlled access to him.

With the decline of the military necessities, more attention could be placed on residential chambers with amenities such as lighter walls, more windows and fireplaces, private rooms, and pleasure gardens. The buildings that once filled the castle yard joined to become either a single courtyard house built around an open yard or a tower house in which rooms were stacked one above another. By the fifteenth century the courtyard house had become the norm for the great dwelling, although the tower house continued in places like Scotland and Ireland. In sophisticated centers, the great military tower was eliminated altogether, except as a ceremonial feature or as a reference to past glories, as seen at Kenilworth (see Figures 10, 27, and 28).

By the fifteenth century, the castle had taken on a symbolic role as a statement of power and status far beyond its military usefulness. As central authority became more important, the government and military role of the castle declined, but the symbolic role increased. The castle's towers and high walls became a visual symbol of the owner's position. The castle, always a setting for the rituals of life, became a stage on which the kings and nobles played their roles with increasing theatricality. Castle architecture always balanced the need for security against the requirements of daily life, the desire for grandeur and ceremonial moments against comfort and convenience. The castle changed from a residential fortress to a fortified palace and finally to a palace whose fortifications were only decorative and symbolic. Castles became show places, spectacles themselves—as, for example, many of the castles in the Loire Valley in France and the halls of Elizabethan England. In the modern world castles gave way to garrison fortresses like Fort McHenry in Baltimore or to command centers like the Pentagon in Washington. Today fantasy castles are still seen in films and amusement parks.

SUGGESTIONS FOR FURTHER READING

Friar, Stephen. *The Sutton Companion to Castles*. Phoenix Mill, UK: Sutton Publishing, 2003.

Le Page, Jean-Denis G. G. *Castles and Fortified Cities of Medieval Europe, an Illustrated History*. Jefferson, NC, and London: McFarland & Company, 2002.

Toy, Sidney. *A History of Fortification from 3000 B.C. to A.D. 1700*. New York: Macmillan, 1955.

Tuulse, Armin. *Castles of the Western World*. Translated by R. P. Girdwood. London: Thames and Hudson, 1958.

CHAPTER 1

THE GREAT TOWER:
NORMAN AND EARLY PLANTAGENET CASTLES

THE NORMANS CONQUER ENGLAND

When William the Conqueror and his Norman warriors swept though England after defeating Harold and his Anglo-Saxon army at Hastings, October 14, 1066, no castles impeded their progress, according to the Anglo-Norman monk Ordericus Vitalis. The Normans came not to plunder but to conquer England. William as king parceled out the Anglo-Saxon lands to his major supporters, instituting in England a political and economic system known today as feudalism.

William's progress through the Anglo-Saxon kingdom was swift and dramatic. He landed at Pevensey, where he used the surviving walls of an ancient Roman fortress to shelter his troops. Then he seized Hastings and built a castle—a hastily erected earthwork topped with timber palisades—to protect his men and ships. William might have brought prefabricated timber buildings with him from Normandy, because the Normans were known to have used such forts; however, no clear evidence exists for such buildings during the first years of the conquest. After defeating the Anglo-Saxons at Hastings, William immediately moved on to Dover. Dover Castle, then as now, commanded the waterway between England and the continent of Europe. In Dover, William would have found the remains of an Iron Age hill fort, a Roman camp and lighthouse, and an Anglo-Saxon church. William ordered the site to be reinforced with ditches and palisades. Turning inland, William arrived at Canterbury, where he rested his troops, who were by then tired and sick. Then he marched on London. In London he built his castle, an earthwork beside the southeast corner of the Roman city wall. This fortification would become the Tower of London.

William had left his wife Matilda in charge of Normandy (Document 44), so he made a quick trip home to make sure all was well, but he returned to England at once to put down a rebellion by the still-powerful Anglo-Saxon earls in the west and north. Suddenly the Danes invaded and burned the castle at York. William drove them out and not only rebuilt York's castle but also added a second. Within six years, between 1066 and 1072, William took control of the country from the English Channel to the border with Scotland and from the fens of East Anglia to the Welsh mountains.

EARLY TIMBER CASTLES

As they captured each territory, William and his men secured their camps with simple earth and timber defenses characteristic of northern Europe (Documents 2 and 3). These wooden structures have disintegrated, but sometimes their earthen mounds survive as rolling hills or picturesque elements in the landscape. Timber castles were especially useful to a warrior king like William the Conqueror who moved rapidly to bring new territories under control. The earth and timber castles could be built quickly, since the newly moved earth did not have to support great weight. Such structures were also relatively cheap because they required no specialized masons and expensive stone. Since the timber building tradition was widespread both in the British Isles and on the continent, the carpenters knew the building techniques. These castles were essentially towers and stockades; they provided garrison headquarters as well as residences.

William had learned the value, as well as the technique, of building and using castles at home in Normandy, where castles and siege warfare had been developed in the ninth and tenth centuries. The strong rule of Charlemagne had given the people of Europe some sense of security, so that Charlemagne's grandson, Charles the Bald, even issued a prohibition in 864 against the building of private fortifications. But intensified Viking raids along the coast of France in the later years of the ninth century forced the people to insist on permission to defend themselves and to fortify their homes. By 869, Charles the Bald rescinded his edict, and the landholders began building walls around their homesteads again. Relative peace returned in 911 when the Viking chieftain Hrolf accepted Christianity and became a vassal of King Charles the Simple. In return

Hrolf received the lands known today as Normandy, and as Rollo, duke of Normandy, he and his Vikings became settlers and builders instead of invaders and raiders.

Ninth-century castles were relatively small and simple affairs designed to safeguard a relatively small number of people and intended as a refuge during times of trouble. A timber tower on its hill or motte, natural or artificial, could serve as a dwelling like the elaborate tower described by Lambert of Ardre (Document 6). The hall and farm buildings stood near the tower. A moat or ditch, earthen ramparts, and stockades surrounded the site that formed the bailey. The owner built the tallest possible tower and the highest walls; he depended on height for observation and defense. Because he expected his enemies to try to enter in the same place he did, he also fortified the gateway to the compound.

The Motte and Bailey Castle

A motte and bailey castle consists of a man-made hill (the motte) supporting a tower and a walled yard (the bailey). The word *motte* is also the source of the word *moat*, or ditch. Early castle builders looked for a natural hill on which to erect a timber tower, but since a hill might not be available where fortifications were needed, they raised a flat-topped, conical earthen mound by digging a circular trench or ditch the desired diameter and heaping up the dirt in the center (Figure 5, Document 12). This ditch not only provided the earth for the motte but also by its depth added to the motte's overall height. Mottes varied in size from about 100 to 300 feet in diameter and may have once stood as high as 100 feet. Thetford, the largest surviving motte in England, has a diameter at the base of about 360 feet and a height of about 80 feet.

As soon as the earth settled, the builders erected a wooden tower on the top of the mound. This tower served as a home for the lord or his castellan (constable, the governor of the castle) and his family and favored retainers, as a lookout post, and as a secure and defensible castle in wartime (Documents 6, 7, and 8). Some mottes had only a circular wall, not a tower. The tower on the motte was called the "great tower." *Donjon*, a fourteenth-century French term (Old French: "lord"), and the sixteenth-century English word *keep* (of unknown origin) are terms commonly used today.

Figure 5. Norman motte, Arundel Castle, England. The motte at Arundel dates to c. 1088. William d'Abini (d. 1176) replaced the wooden structure on its top with the stone tower we see today. Like Windsor Castle, Arundel had a bailey on each side of the motte. Most of the castle buildings seen today were built in the 1890s. *Photograph: Karen Leider.*

The Bailey

The top of the motte was a rather constricted space, and the timber tower could not house all the people who needed protection, so a second trench and embankment were dug around or beside the motte to enclose a yard called the bailey (also called a "ward" in England). Palisades (walls of upright timbers) on the crest of these embankments added to their strength and effectiveness. Inside the bailey, timber and turf buildings sheltered men, animals, and supplies. By the twelfth century the number of buildings inside the walls increased and might include a great hall, a chapel, a chamber block and additional sleeping quarters, a kitchen, barns and stables, storerooms, and—since the settlement had to be self-sufficient—a well or some provision for water, a smithy for repairing weapons, a mill to grind the grain, and an oven to bake the daily bread. Although to us the castle with its many buildings and inhabitants may seem like a village, it functions differently. City walls were built as a collective defensive system; the castle was the property and home of an individual family and the place where the lord held court and administered the surrounding territory.

The Need for Castles

Wherever they went, William and his Norman lieutenants built castles. About 170 great vassals came to England with William. When the king rewarded his followers with grants of land, they also assumed the responsibility for its defense, so each built one or more castles. William and his men had several reasons for building castles. As hostile invaders they had to fortify their dwellings and camps in order to hold the territory and provide security for themselves. Their castles also secured borders and coastlines against other invaders and controlled the movement of people and goods at key transportation centers such as fords, bridges, and passes and along major roads.

Alas, Wooden Castles Burn

Motte and bailey castles had serious disadvantages in a siege. Timber walls and towers were especially vulnerable to fire, and a castle that could be set on fire with torches or scorching arrows provided only a short-term solution to the need for defense. Obviously, walls had to be converted to stone as soon as possible, but years had to pass before an artificial mound had settled enough to bear heavy stone masonry. Where a natural hill was available, especially a cliff beside a river that formed a natural water barrier, stone towers and walls were being built by the end of the eleventh century.

THE FIRST STONE CASTLES

Stone towers appeared early in the Loire River valley. The massive ruin at Langeais, recently dated 992, was once a broad tower with four corner turrets. Today it stands in the park of a fifteenth-century chateau. Not far off, at Loches, the tower is the earliest surviving great tower to combine within its walls a hall, the lord's chamber, and a chapel. Recent analysis of the wood used in the original building has dated this tower between 1012 and 1035. Meanwhile, in England, as we have seen, during the first years after the Norman invasion, William and his men depended on hastily built earth and timber defenses but replaced the wooden castles with stone as soon as the earth had compacted. Masonry required good stone quarries and quarry men, powerful ox teams to transport the material, and skilled stonemasons to construct the walls and vaults. Stone castles became a heavy burden on the people (Documents 13–19).

The Castle at Loches

The huge stone tower at Loches stood 108 feet high, and its ground plan had an exterior dimension of eighty-three feet by fifty feet, six inches. The tower had four floors, each of which consisted of a single room. The ground floor must have served as storage space, because it had no windows, only open slits for air circulation. The principal floor contained the great hall, which was used for public events. This hall was an imposing place for both ceremony and government. Here the lord sat in state with members of his household and his guests. By the twelfth century the household consisted of the family and the officials who served the lord and conducted his business—the constable or castellan who governed the castle when the lord was away, the steward and butler who provided food and drink, the chamberlain who looked after the clothes and other possessions, and the chancellor who kept written records and supervised the chapel. The constable and the marshal were responsible for security, the troops, and the stables.

The hall was a splendid room with practical amenities such as fireplaces and garderobes (latrines), which were built into the thickness of the wall. The forebuilding, a fortified structure, enclosed the outside stairs and controlled access to the great hall. At Loches the forebuilding also housed the chapel. The third floor in the tower may have been a semiprivate hall, which was reached from the hall by means of stairs built into the wall. Finally the top floor provided additional living space and was reached by spiral stairs. The few windows were limited to the upper floors. Cut through the massive walls, window enclosures formed spaces that resembled small rooms.

The tower at Loches is built in an early Romanesque style with pilaster and half-column decorated exterior walls, small round-headed win-

Figure 6. Great tower, Rochester Castle, England. A great blocky mass, at 115 feet with 10-foot-tall corner turrets, the great tower of Rochester is the tallest surviving example of a Norman tower in England. *Photograph: Marilyn Stokstad.*

dows, and fine stone masonry. Its imposing height and high quality stonework suggest that it was built not only to withstand attacks but also to impress the people living in the surrounding countryside with the power of the owner.

The Castle at Rochester

The castle at Rochester, a vital position where the road to London crossed the Medway River, still gives an excellent idea of a Norman great tower (Figure 6). The ancient Romans had recognized the strategic importance of the site and had built a fort. Later, the Anglo-Saxons built their cathedral east of the Roman fort. William the Conqueror, in turn, appropriated the surviving Roman walls and placed his tower in the southwest corner of the Roman camp. Gundolf, the bishop of Rochester from 1076/77 to 1108, rebuilt the castle between 1087 and 1089, but the huge tower we see today dates from the reign of King Henry I (1100–35), who gave the castle and permission to rebuild a tower to Archbishop Corbeil of Canterbury (1123–36). The tower was certainly finished by 1141 although the cylindrical tower at the southeast corner dates from the restoration after a siege in 1216.

Early Norman great towers were rectangular buildings usually three or four stories high, with massive rectangular towers rising from buttresses clasping the corners. At Rochester the tower had four floors: a ground floor used for storage, a first-floor room entered from the stair in the fore-building, a main hall of double height, and an upper floor. A wall divided each floor into two parts, and spiral stairs in the corners provided access to the floors. The principal room was on the second floor, with private rooms on the upper floors; fireplaces, garderobes, and small chambers were built in the thickness of the wall. Admission to the great hall at Rochester castle was by means of a complex and imposing stair and fore-building. Stairs begin on the west side of the tower, rise along the wall, turn the corner, and continue into a turret to an ante-room at the side of the principal hall. A drawbridge also protected the portal. The unusual eight-foot width of the stair suggests that it had a ceremonial function. A chapel occupied the upper floor of the forebuilding. Here, paired windows lit the impressive carved portal of the chapel. In contrast to Loches, Rochester was the first Norman tower to emphasize height rather than mass. The great tower at Rochester stood about 125 feet tall, including the corner turrets, and had a square plan with an exterior measurement of seventy feet. Corner and wall buttresses strengthen the walls.

On the principal floor, wide arches rather than a wall divided the space into two halls (Figure 7). These halls were two stories (twenty-seven feet) high, with window embrasures in the thickness of the upper wall. Wall passages led to these window rooms and to the chapel over the entrance. The principal hall was richly decorated. The arches are carved with chevrons, and columns with scalloped capitals flank large windows that could be closed by shutters. An upper floor provided private rooms for the lord or his castellan and the family. This floor had small chambers, as well as fireplaces and garderobes, built into the walls. In the center of each floor, superimposed openings created an open shaft for a windlass on the roof, which lifted materials such as food or rocks and other

Figure 7. Great tower, Rochester Castle, England, interior. Seen from the top of the wall, the interior stonework of the castle lies exposed. A masonry wall divided the building into two sections. The arches and piers of the principal hall can be seen at the lower left, and the holes for the beams supporting the wooden floors cross the wall at a higher level. *Photograph: Marilyn Stokstad.*

weapons from the storage and service areas in the ground-floor room to the halls and the roof. At the top of the walls a crenellated wall-walk gave the soldiers space to watch and if necessary shoot arrows or drop missiles on the enemy. The castle garrison could build wooden platforms and walls, called hoardings, out from the top of the wall to give themselves extra protected space. The great tower stood in a walled bailey, which today forms a public park. The peaceful expanse of grass belies its original use.

Originally everyone lived—ate and slept, squabbled, and entertained themselves—in the hall. Only the castellan and his family might have a place to themselves. In the living rooms, charcoal braziers provided some warmth, and open fires or wall fireplaces created smoke-filled rooms (chimneys came later). Sanitation was an important concern to owners of castles, who insisted on having adequate garderobes easily reached from the principal rooms. People bathed in portable tubs. Because of the danger of fire, kitchens and ovens were usually separate buildings in the bailey. Shelters for the garrison, the servants, and the horses and livestock were also in the bailey. A chapel could be an independent building in the bailey, or might be placed in the tower itself, as in the Tower of London, or—as at Rochester—in the forebuilding.

The castle had to be self-sufficient. Wars usually consisted of sieges in which the aggressor invested (that is, cut off supplies to the castle) and tried to batter down the castle walls or starve its people into submission. Battering down or tunneling under the walls was usually less effective than starvation. Since early armies were raised by feudal levies and the troops were undisciplined and forced to live off the land, time was on the side of the people in the castle. Tenants usually owed forty days' service a year in wartime, but only twenty during peace. A feudal army might simply go home when their time had been served. The castle garrison did not need to be very large, and in a well-provisioned castle with a secure water supply it could hope to outlast the siege. (For the siege of Rochester, see Chapter 2.)

The White Tower of London

The most famous Norman great tower today is the White Tower of London (Figure 8). The castle was begun in the 1070s and construction continued into the 1090s. To improve his original ditch and bank de-

Figure 8. The White Tower, Tower of London, exterior of Chapel of St. John. The white plastered walls of the White Tower were also enriched with pilaster-buttresses joined by arches. The corner turret at the right was slightly enlarged to accommodate a formal staircase, and the large semicircular tower at the left is the outer wall of the apse of the Chapel of St. John. *Photograph: Karen Leider.*

fenses in London, William the Conqueror put Bishop Gundolph of Rochester in charge of the building project. The building we see today is twelfth century and later. (A study of the wood gives a date in the early twelfth century for the upper part of the tower.) The kings lavished money on the castle in 1129–30, 1171–72, and the 1180s and recorded the annual expenses in official royal accounts (known as Pipe Rolls). In 1190 Richard the Lion Hearted spent enormous sums on a new ditch, bank, and curtain wall. Today the castle has been heavily restored and is entirely surrounded by later buildings, but it still exerts a sense of grim strength.

With plastered and whitewashed walls, the White Tower lived up to its name. Since it stood beside the river Thames, not on a hill or motte, its lower walls had to be very thick, between fourteen and fifteen feet thick at the base. The tower had a rectangular plan, 97 feet by 118 feet. Four pilaster buttresses (projecting masonry panels) enriched each outer wall, dividing the walls into bays (compartments or units of space), and corner buttresses extended upward to form turrets at the corners. The windows have been enlarged, and a top story added. The forebuilding that once held the stair has been destroyed and replaced today with wooden stairs. The tower had only this one entrance, so everyone and everything—even supplies going to the basement—came through this door.

Since there are few accommodations for a household, the White Tower may have been designed as a public and administrative building rather than as a residence. It has two levels of state rooms. A wall pierced with wide arches divides each floor into two halls of unequal size. Spiral stairs join the floors, and in one corner an unusually wide stair must have been used for formal processional entrances. A chapel dedicated to St. John replaces one corner turret. Its apse forms a semicircular tower (Figure 9). Romanesque in style and construction, the chapel's cylindrical columns divide the space into a nave and aisles and support a barrel vault. The groin-vaulted aisles support galleries, which join a wall passage running all the way around the tower at the upper window level. On the upper floor the rooms are luxurious, with large windows, fireplaces, and garderobes.

Windsor and Arundel Castles

At Windsor Castle (see Figure 2) and Arundel (see Figure 5) in southern England the dramatic height of a motte can still be admired. These castle mounds were first topped by palisades without towers, which were rebuilt first in stone and then as towers in the twelfth century. At Arundel, the home of the dukes of Norfolk since the sixteenth century, most of the buildings within the castle walls date from the 1890s. At Windsor, Sir Jeffry Wyatville, the architect of King George IV, added a thirty-

Figure 9. Chapel of St. John, Tower of London, interior. An arcade on massive round piers divides the space into a nave and side aisles. The second-story gallery opening into the nave continues around the entire tower and provides access to the gallery from the principal rooms. *Photograph: Anna Leider.*

three-foot-high stone wall to the low Norman great tower to create its present imposing height. The machicolations are also Wyatville's work. Beyond the motte, the castle buildings we admire today are the result of nineteenth-century enthusiasm for the Middle Ages and the rebuilding of medieval architecture.

The Impact of the Crusades

Beginning at the end of the eleventh century, the Crusades introduced Europeans to sophisticated Byzantine and Muslim military architecture and ushered in a new phase of castle building. As long as wars were fought with poorly trained and undisciplined troops, and when battles were short, bloody encounters between mobs going at each other in hand-to-hand combat, the great tower and its walled enclosure made an effective castle. As siege techniques and equipment changed and troops of archers and teams of siege engineers joined knights trained for single combat, the castle design had to change to meet the new challenge (see Chapter 2). Pembroke, on the south coast of Wales, was founded by Normans in 1093–94 (see Figures 3 and 4). The great round tower from the end of the twelfth century shows a marked improvement in military engineering over the square plan of earlier towers. With no corners to batter or mine and of masonry throughout, the round tower was a significant improvement on the earlier cubical buildings.

The Burden of Castle Building

All this castle building placed a heavy burden on the kingdom. The nobles raided and harassed each other. Castles changed hands regularly, often through trickery. As rivals engaged in a constant round of destruction, they forced their people to work on the castle maintenance and rebuilding (Documents 12–19). The common people, forced to do the work, hated the castle builders.

EARLY PLANTAGENET CASTLES

By the time Henry II Plantagenet (r. 1154–89) was crowned king of England in 1154, baronial castles outnumbered royal castles. A tough, dynamic ruler, Henry began to rectify the situation at once. In the north, King Malcolm of Scotland surrendered to him, giving Henry significant castles in Scotland and in the border territory. Many older castles like Windsor were strengthened. At Dover the masonry great tower and forebuilding were built in the 1180s, and concentric walls with half-round towers were added by Richard the Lion Hearted seventeen years later.

Figure 10. Great tower, Kenilworth Castle, England. The square tower with corner turrets continued to be built throughout the twelfth century. The large windows seen today at Kenilworth are the result of later modernization that turned the castle into a palatial residence. *Photograph: Marilyn Stokstad.*

Kenilworth and Pembroke Castles

At Kenilworth, where later building would make the castle one of the most complex expressions of a courtly age (see Chapter 4), a massive tower was built about 1122 by Geoffrey de Clinton, who acquired the land for a castle and park (Figure 10). These tower strongholds continued to be built longer than one might expect, considering their disadvantages as dwellings.

Kenilworth became a royal castle in 1173 when King Henry II acquired it. Henry repaired the great tower and subsidiary buildings in 1184. Work continued in 1190–93 during the reign of Richard the Lion Hearted. Built of sandstone in well-cut ashlar blocks, Kenilworth Castle followed the traditional cubical Norman design but had large rectangular turrets, which seem to clasp the corners. Each of these turrets had its special function. The southwest tower contained the entrance (and later a forebuilding was added to conceal the actual door); the northeast tower had a spiral staircase providing access to all floors; and the northwest tower contained the garderobes. A fighting gallery ran along the wall head.

The round towers were the answer to many problems. At Pembroke about 1189, Earl William Marshall built a splendid round tower (see Figure 4). In that year he married a wealthy heiress who provided the resources required for building an imposing and functional castle. A round tower had fewer blind spots and needed less masonry, and furthermore needed little buttressing. The tower at Pembroke Castle is not only large but also elegantly appointed. Barrel vaults and groined vaults were both used instead of wooden floors, and the uppermost room is covered by a dome. The double-light windows with dogtooth ornament set in deep embrasures form window seats. The earl and countess resided at Pembroke until he left for Ireland in 1207.

Challenges and Architectural Solutions

Great towers looked imposing, but after a time they proved to be not very practical either for living or for fighting. During a siege, comfort and convenience were irrelevant, but during peacetime, living in the tower could be unduly complicated. Stacked rooms in the towers made movement through the building difficult, and the narrow spiral staircases in the corner turrets weakened the masonry at its most vulnerable spot. Furthermore, with the defense concentrated in a single tower, no matter how strongly built, the garrison had little flexibility during the siege. The rectangular building had a further disadvantage: a straight wall was difficult to defend because of the blind spots, especially at the base of the wall. Defenders had to risk their lives when they leaned out over the wall top to see what was happening. The crenels on the wall-walk were not sufficient, and wooden galleries (hoardings) had to be built out at the top of the wall in order to defend the wall (wall-walks and hoardings can be seen in Figures 12 and 22). Windows were needed for light and air, but they weakened the wall and so were often reduced to slits on the exterior. These arrow slits did not permit the archers to see the ground. By the end of the twelfth century, the builders of castles at Pembroke and Kenilworth perfected arrow slits by making sloping embrasures that permitted archers to shoot down at attackers on the ground.

A very wide moat, such as the artificial lake and swamp (the "Great Mere") created at Kenilworth, or a natural water barrier, such as the river Thames in London, effectively defended walls and countered attempts at mining. A good moat or ditch had to be too wide and deep to jump, wade, fill, or bridge. To reach the entrance, drawbridges were used, although the size of available timbers limited the size of the gap that could be bridged. Since doors were vulnerable places, elaborate defenses concentrated there. A sliding portcullis was an effective deterrent, but it required space for a counterpoise or windlass. Gatehouses solved this problem. Finally, a small semisecret back door or postern was usually built in the bailey walls. Also known as a "sally port," the gate permitted the defenders to exit, engage in a brief battle, and return to the safety of their castle.

The Great Tower Becomes Obsolete

The last of the great tower castles may be Richard the Lion Hearted's French castle Chateau Gaillard (see Chapter 2), built after his capture and ransom in 1192–93. In spite of the terrible strain that Richard's ransom had placed on the English treasury, the castle was built rapidly. After Richard's death the strength of the tower, the double walls and ditches, and the complex forebuildings did not save the garrison at Chateau Gaillard. The castle fell to the French king in 1204.

As castle design evolved, the great tower was eventually replaced by walled enclosures, which permitted more effective use of troops and better living conditions. The future of castle design lay with the curtain wall, that is, a wall "hung" like a curtain between towers, each of which functioned like a keep. The builders of the walls of Constantinople had seen the virtues of wall towers and curtain walls centuries earlier, and western crusaders who passed through Constantinople had the opportunity of studying these ancient fortifications.

Halls and Chamber Blocks

The hall, not the tower, became the principal element of domestic architecture. This architectural form served as a royal residence, a hunting lodge, or simply a rural manor house. The king held court in the great halls built at palaces like Westminster and Winchester. The hall, a large, long, rectangular building of either one or two stories, was soon integrated into the total castle design. The three-aisled ground floor hall was the usual form in early days. Later the principal room, used for banquets and official functions, was raised on a vaulted undercroft. The entrance was at one of the narrow ends, and opposite the entrance, the lord's throne-like chair and the high table stood on a raised dais. Halls could be built of masonry or wood or a combination of both. The most splendid halls resembled the nave of a large church. The Normans, as great church builders, had experience in erecting huge masonry buildings; for example, Winchester Cathedral had a nave and aisles that measure 265 feet, 9 inches by 85 feet, 4 inches (81 × 26 m.). The surviving thirteenth-century royal hall at Winchester was 110 feet long. William Rufus' late eleventh-century hall at Westminster (probably the largest hall in western Europe) was 240 feet by 67 feet. No one knows how Westminster Hall was roofed, although it may have had wooden pillars and arches supporting a wooden roof. It was painted brilliant red and blue.

The Normans also built residential buildings known as chamber blocks within the castle walls. The chamber block usually had two stories; the lower floor was a public space and the upper floor was used by the family. The building had such amenities as garderobes and fireplaces and might also include a chapel. Doors and windows in the chamber block might be decorated with elegant carvings. By the end of the twelfth century, wool and linen hangings on the inner walls would have cut drafts and added to the comfort and of luxury of the room.

To summarize, the principal buildings required by a great lord and his household consisted of the great tower (later called the keep or donjon), a hall, and a chamber block—three separate or loosely joined buildings—plus all the necessary support buildings—barns, stables, and workshops. A defensive system of walls, towers, and ditches surrounded the complex, which functioned as a unit to form the twelfth-century castle.

SUGGESTIONS FOR FURTHER READING

Fernie, Eric. *The Architecture of Norman England.* Oxford: Oxford University Press, 2000.

Liddiard, Robert, ed. *Anglo-Norman Castles.* Woodbridge, Suffolk, UK: Boydell Press, 2003.

CHAPTER 2

THE CASTLE AS FORTRESS:
THE CASTLE AND SIEGE WARFARE

Warfare had become endemic in eleventh- and twelfth-century Europe. Castle building used up the resources of the land as every landholder from the king and great nobles to the small landholders fortified their dwellings. Constant skirmishing, brigandage, and open warfare at home and abroad meant that people poured vast resources into training and equipping warriors and building castles and siege machines. The motte and bailey castle with its great tower, as the keep or donjon is called in medieval documents, was admirably suited as a defense against local skirmishes. The castle was also a symbolic expression of its owner's power and pride (Figure 11). During the twelfth and thirteenth centuries, as kings and nobles tried to form larger estates and nations, they built massive stone castles.

Cities and towns sought to define and defend their borders by building walls and fortified gates. Even churches and monasteries had defensive walls. At the city of Avila, Spain, the cathedral apse formed one of the most powerful towers in the encircling walls, and in northwest Spain, the cathedral of Santiago de Compostela had to withstand a siege. Even monasteries like the Abbey of St. Denis just north of Paris in France had crenellated walls. In the nineteenth century the French architect Viollet-le-Duc restored the walls and towers of Carcassonne. Today the old city gives us a romanticized idea of medieval fortifications (Figures 11, 12, and 13).

The emergence of Islam as an international religion and the success of Muslim armies also energized Christian forces and drew them into wars

Figure 11. Castle of the Counts, Carcassonne, France. Although the entrance into the Castle of the Counts is within the fortified city, it has independent defenses, including a ditch once crossed by a drawbridge and a pair of round defensive towers. At the top of the crenellated towers, holes for the ends of beams supporting wooden hoardings can be seen. *Photograph: Karen Leider.*

Figure 12. Wall and towers with hoardings, Carcassonne, France. As restored by Viollet-le-Duc, this section of the walls represents the city as it would have been seen when prepared for war. Hoardings were temporary wooden platforms and walls that doubled or tripled the space available for the defenders on the top of the walls. *Photograph: Karen Leider.*

Figure 13. The walls and the lists, Carcassonne, France. The strongest castles and a few cities had double walls, a system perfected by the Byzantine builders of the walls of Constantinople. Archers on the high inner walls could shoot over the heads of men on the outer wall. The space between the walls, called the list, was used for exercise, training, and tournaments. *Photograph: Karen Leider.*

where tactics—and castles—became increasingly sophisticated. Jerusalem as the holy city of three faiths—Jewish, Christian, and Muslim—remained the focus of western European thought and pilgrimage even though the city and the holiest sites in Christendom lay in Muslim hands. Muslims also controlled northern Africa and the Iberian Peninsula. In the ninth century St. James miraculously appeared in northern Spain to turn the tide of battle, leading Christian forces to victory and so beginning the Christian reconquest of the Iberian Peninsula.

At the end of the eleventh century (1095) Pope Urban II traveled through France preaching a crusade to liberate Jerusalem. French, Flemish, German, and English nobles joined in the enterprise. The First Crusade left in 1096, Christians captured Antioch in 1098, and by July 1099 Jerusalem again lay in Christian hands (Documents 29–32). The crusaders established Christian kingdoms in Palestine and Syria, ruled by the warriors Bohemund in Antioch and Godfrey of Bouillon and then Baldwin in Jerusalem. But Muslims captured Christian Edessa in 1144, and in 1147 the Christians mounted the Second Crusade. When the Muslim leader Saladin (r. 1174–93) recaptured Jerusalem in 1187, the kings of western Europe—Frederick Barbarossa of Germany (r. 1152–90), Philip Augustus of France (r. 1180–1223), and Richard the Lion Hearted of England (r. 1189–99)—rallied the Christian forces yet again. The Third Crusade ended in a truce. Mythmakers glorified the leaders: Saladin and Richard became models for the perfect knight. Frederick, who drowned before even reaching the Holy Land, supposedly was only sleeping until called again to save the German people. Only Philip Augustus was not glorified by the troubadours, and only he profited from the Crusades. As an astute politician, Philip Augustus emerged as the leader of the ever-larger and more powerful nation of France.

The Crusades led to rapid developments in castle design as the combatants studied each other's buildings and weapons. The most sophisticated and skilled military engineers had been the Byzantines. As early as the "Golden Age" of Theodosius and Justinian in the fifth and sixth centuries, the Byzantines knew the advantages of double walls staggered in height, independent projecting wall towers, round rather than squared-off corners, masonry built up in alternating bands of stone and brick, and heavily fortified gateways. Christians and Muslims alike had the mighty walls of Constantinople before them as models (see "Overview: Castles in Context"). Muslim military engineers paid special attention to gateways and invented the most complex turns and traps, murder holes and arrow slots, portcullises and drawbridges. The crusaders, as invaders without a local support system, became painfully aware of the problems of supplying their forces, and they added huge water reservoirs and storage facilities within their castle walls. When these warriors returned to their homelands, they took with them the experience gained in the Holy Land. In the twelfth century, sophisticated defense systems appeared throughout Europe.

Intermittent warfare between Christians and Muslims in the Iberian Peninsula, Syria, and Palestine also led to cultural as well as military exchanges. Crusaders returning to their homes in western Europe brought back new ideas of luxurious living (spices, perfume, carpets, and pieces of richly inlaid metal), new plants (rice, lemons, melons, and apricots), and new technology (water wheels, windmills, and chimneys). The knightly order of the Templars established a rudimentary international banking operation leading to new opportunities for merchants and rulers. Finally, the experience of travel led to further exploration, and gradually European society changed.

THE CASTLE IN ACTION: THE DEFENSE

The siege warfare of the Middle Ages consisted of blockading the castle in hopes of destroying it or taking it over for one's own use. In peacetime castles controlled the surrounding land, but when hostilities broke out they provided passive resistance and served as a base of operations. Constant skirmishing and outright warfare continued through the thirteenth century and led to steady improvement in offensive weapons and in castle design.

In the simplest terms, a lord and landholder secured his home with walls whose height and thickness frustrated a direct assault. His enemies could surround his castle and by cutting off supplies could hope to starve him into surrender. Since armies were unreliable and men served only for a specific period, the besiegers might simply go home to look after their own affairs. In this situation, the defenders of a well-built and well-stocked castle with a secure water supply had the advantage. In short, the garrison relied on the passive strength of their castle's high, thick walls. They might make an occasional sally from a postern gate, but to win, they had to rely on the defection of besieging troops or relief by the arrival of a friendly army.

The Walls

During the course of the eleventh and twelfth centuries, walls became higher and thicker, often sloping out at the bottom to counter attacks with battering rams. The parapet on the outer side of the walk along the top of the wall was notched with crenellations—that is, crenels (low walls) alternating with merlons (higher walls), behind which men on the wall-walk could seek protection (see the crenellated wall-walk at Aigues

Mortes, Figure 22). The merlons could be pierced with arrow loops, holes through which archers could shoot while still being protected by the merlon. Such walls did not permit adequate observation or defense of the entire wall, because the men could not see the bottom of the wall without leaning over the crenels and exposing themselves to the enemy's death-dealing arrows and rocks. The addition of towers built out in front of the wall and galleries over the top of the wall solved this problem. The wall-walk could be developed into a full-scale fighting gallery. Temporary wooden galleries, known as hoardings, doubled or tripled the space available for the defenders at the top of the wall (see Figure 12). Beams or brackets supported the hoardings and permitted holes in the floor through which the defenders could observe the wall and its base, shoot their arrows, or drop stones and other missiles. Brief forays (sallies) outside the walls helped to keep up the defenders' morale.

The Gate

Castle builders considered the entrance to be the most vulnerable part of the castle, and they lavished attention on elaborate defenses for the portal. Muslim military engineers were especially adept at building complex gatehouses, and western crusaders learned from them and developed their own elaborate fortified gates. The portal itself had a heavy wooden door, often reinforced with metal, and one or more wood or metal grilles, called portcullises (port—gate, coulis—a sliding door), which could be dropped or slid into place from the upper chambers of the gatehouse. The passage through the gatehouse was also carefully designed—sharp turns prevented the use of a battering ram or a rush of troops, while holes in the vaults ("murder holes") permitted guards to shoot or drop missiles on people below and also to pour water on any fires the attackers might build against the wooden doors. One of the finest gatehouses in the west was planned for Caernarfon Castle in Wales (see Chapter 3) where (if it had been finished) five doors and six portcullises, as well as turns and murder holes, defended the entrance. The gatehouse also had rooms for a permanent troop of guards. Since the castle was usually surrounded by some kind of ditch or moat, which might be either dry or filled with water, a bridge that could be raised or turned also defended the entrance. A raised drawbridge added its weight and thickness to the entrance portal. A small fortress called a barbican, built in front of the gatehouse, reinforced the effectiveness of the defense. Its towers and walls formed a trap for the unwanted and unwary. From the walls and towers of the bar-bican, defenders could fire down on attackers, turning their rush on the entrance into a murderous slaughter.

THE CASTLE IN ACTION: THE ATTACK

When an attacking force laid siege to a castle, they used techniques and weapons not unlike those developed by the ancient Romans. First they surrounded the castle in order to cut off all avenues of escape and resupply. They also built a camp ringed by ditches and palisades to se-cure their own position. Then they built siege engines—great stone-throwing devices—which they hoped would break down the castle walls. Although the knights' chivalric code gave pride of place in warfare to a charge on horseback with lance or to hand-to-hand combat with swords, military engineers skilled in the mechanics of offensive engines had to first break through the walls. To breach the walls the army used batter-ing rams, various kinds of projectiles, and mines. In other words they tried to go through, over, or under the walls (Document 25).

Battering Rams

To be effective, the war machines needed level ground facing the cas-tle walls. So castle builders positioned their buildings on cliffs or sur-rounded them with natural defenses or ditches. Many powerful castles had water-filled moats that were as wide as lakes or ponds. The attack-ing army had to begin its siege by filling the ditch or moat, perhaps break-ing dams or diverting streams to do so. Then a causeway had to be built over which battering rams and siege towers could be rolled into place. A battering ram—a huge metal-tipped pole hung in a sling and protected by a roof—might be so large that it required a hundred men to swing it against a wall or tower (Document 26). Small rams could be operated by a dozen men and used in confined spaces such as gatehouses.

As the ram pounded the wall, the defenders tried to absorb the shock by hanging bundles of wool or straw in front of the wall. The defenders also tried to catch the ram with grappling hooks and lift it into a verti-cal position rendering it useless. Less dramatic was the process of sapping, in which the attackers attempted to bore through the walls rather than batter them down. The men operating the equipment were vulnerable to missiles, fire, or hot pitch thrown at them by the castle's defenders, so they worked under a moveable shed (penthouse) whose roof was covered with earth and hides. This shield was called a "turtle" because of its shell or a "cat" because of its sneaky approach.

Stone-Throwing Machines

Medieval artillery consisted of three types of stone-throwing machines (*petraria*): the *ballista*, which worked on the principles of the slingshot or catapult; the *mangonel*, which worked by torsion; and the *trebuchet*, or beam, which consisted of a sling and counterweight. These machines hurled rocks of various sizes, making ammunition a renewable resource. Their range was 90–300 yards. The ballista shot bolts like a large cross-bow. The huge mangonel could throw stones weighing over 200 pounds a distance of over 200 yards—more than twice the length of a modern football field (Figure 14). The most powerful and accurate weapon (far more effective than the early cannons) was the trebuchet, which had a range of about 300 yards. The trebuchet consisted of a beam on a pivot, having a bucket weighted with stones and earth at one end and a sling for the missile at the other end. Operated by a team of up to sixty men, the trebuchet fired huge boulders that shook the walls and broke through the crenellations and machicolations. Its sling could also be filled with rubbish, garbage, and even dead men and animals, which it slung over castle walls to insult, terrify, spread disease, and infect the water and food supplies. A trebuchet required almost half an hour to load and fire. The trebuchet was invented late in the twelfth century; its earliest use in England was by barons against King John in 1215–16. In the next century Edward I of England was so proud of his trebuchet (named "War Wolf") that in 1309 he had a reviewing platform built so that the queen and her ladies could watch the machine in action during a siege in Scotland. None of these war machines survive, although modern reenactors have built and tested them. At the castle of Chinon one can see a modern reproduction set out in the ditch between the forebuilding and the main castle. The medieval city of Les Baux in southern France has a collection of reconstructed siege weapons.

Figure 14. Mangonel (modern reconstruction), Castle of Chinon, France. Look-ing down into the ditch, which was part of the defenses of the castle, one sees a giant catapult, or mangonel. Today's military historians and re-enacters have constructed and demonstrated many medieval engines of war. *Photograph: Karen Leider.*

Tunnels

The least glamorous but often the most effective way of breaching the walls was by mining, that is, tunneling under the wall (Document 27). Obviously, mining was used where a castle was not built on solid rock or surrounded by water. The miners propped up the tunnel with timber as they dug so that, when the wood was burned, the unsupported wall came crashing down. The miners might tie kindling to pigs, set the poor beasts alight, and drive them into the tunnel to ignite the timbers. The fat of the burning pigs increased the intensity of the fire.

To defend against mining, the castle occupants excavated their own tunnel, a technique known as countermining. They could either break through to the rival tunnel and engage in underground combat, or they could light fires and drive the smoke into their opponent's tunnel, mak-ing work impossible.

The Siege Tower

The most spectacular and prestigious siege engine was the belfry or moveable tower (Documents 28 and 39). Only kings and great lords could afford such an expensive piece of woodwork. These towers must have been masterpieces of carpentry, for they had to be as tall as the castle's towers and walls. After filling the ditches and moats the men hauled the finished tower across the causeway and into place beside the wall. In theory, the knights climbed to the upper platform, a drawbridge was dropped from the tower to the castle wall, and the attackers rushed out to engage in hand-to-hand combat. This was the kind of battle for which the knights had trained since childhood. But problems are obvious. Although wet hides made the towers almost fireproof, they could be set on fire, turning them into ovens that roasted the men inside. They could also be toppled over, crushing their users.

Scaling the Walls

The final assault on the castle usually depended on breaching the walls, but it could also be achieved by simply climbing the wall. Scaling ladders and ropes might be used beside or in place of siege towers. Attached by grappling hooks to the walls, they could be countered by men at the top of the wall who pushed the ladders off with poles, or cut the ropes, or simply chopped off the hands of those climbing when they reached the top of the walls. Ladders might be brought up to the wall in pieces, as was the plan in a sneak attack on Edinburgh Castle in the eighteenth century. This attack failed when one of the men failed to show up with his section of the ladder. The plotters tried to scale the wall anyway by using the sections they did have, but their ladder did not reach the top of the wall. Such demonstrations of human frailty and incompetence balance tales of daring and skill.

Knights

The mounted knights formed the heavy cavalry; we might think of them as armored divisions. Battles in the open field lasted a single day and if possible were fought in good weather. Tactics were simple; the knights in squadrons (usually of ten) charged with lances set, followed by hand-to-hand combat. Knights required a team of squires and servants to assist them in arming and to care for armor and weapons. They also needed a stable of horses—the huge specially trained war horses known as the destriers, but also riding horses and pack animals. The goal of a warrior was not to kill but to capture and hold his enemy for ransom and to acquire the enemy's valuable armor, horses, and other loot. Military men made their living by capturing and ransoming prisoners and looting the battlefield and countryside. Capture, not killing, paid off.

Archers

A corps of archers using the long bow (between five and six feet long) and arrows or the crossbow and bolts supported the knights. (In modern terms, they were the infantry.) Fast and maneuverable, longbowmen were very effective in the open field. Working as a team, they could shoot thousands of arrows almost simultaneously. A skilled English archer could shoot between twelve and fifteen arrows a minute with a range of over 300 yards. Men using the slow but more powerful crossbow, with its deadly armor-piercing bolts, had to fire from a shielded position. A crossbowman could shoot only a single bolt to the longbowman's five or six arrows. The crossbow had a range of 370 to 380 yards, although modern claims have been made for shots of 450 yards.

The Surrender

Very few castles were taken by direct assault. Starvation and disease reduced a garrison to the point where they had to surrender or die (Document 40). Chivalric courtesy and elaborate rules surrounded the surrender of a castle—agreements which might or might not be honored by the victors (Documents 36 and 37). For example, the castellan might agree to surrender the castle if relief or reinforcements did not arrive within a certain period of time. Under these circumstances the defending force might be allowed to leave with their arms and honor intact. But often the victorious army failed to keep to the agreement of surrender and slaughtered the entire castle guard. Usually the castellan or lord of the castle left the castle for prison or execution (Document 34).

After a long siege the defeated forces might be so debilitated by starvation and disease that they died shortly after the siege was lifted anyway. Treachery was always a possibility, and many castle and city gates were opened by people who expected to receive large rewards for their treachery. Ingenious tricks and disguises also played a part (Documents 43 and 53).

Although castles were often turned into prisons in the eighteenth and nineteenth centuries, medieval prisons were small. Writers of romantic fiction have made much of dungeons and torture, but medieval justice was usually direct and swift. Traitors were usually killed before they could escape to enjoy their reward. The only prisoners worth keeping were the wealthy nobles who were held for ransom. For them the great tower made an excellent and secure prison (Documents 37 and 41). Important captives lived in luxury; King John of France lived in a London palace, hunted in the royal preserves, and was not eager to return to France.

CHATEAU GAILLARD: RICHARD THE LION HEARTED'S CASTLE AND ITS HORRIBLE END

Richard the Lion Hearted, who became king of England in 1189, had inherited Aquitaine (western France) from his mother Eleanor and Normandy and Anjou—and England—from his father Henry. As Duke of Normandy and Anjou, Richard was a vassal of the king of France, but he controlled more land in France than did the French king. Although Richard had been an ally of Philip Augustus in the Third Crusade, in 1192 he went to war with the king over his French lands. Richard built Chateau Gaillard (he called it the "cocky castle") on a cliff above the Seine north of Paris to defend his claims to Normandy (Figure 15). He began his castle in 1196 and boasted that he finished it in a year (in fact it may never have been completely finished). Having experienced the advantages and defects of the great crusader castles, Richard put all his expertise to work in the design of his Norman fortress.

Richard chose an excellent site, in the territory of the archbishop of Rouen, who objected strenuously until Richard paid him a handsome sum for the land. The site is a narrow plateau, about 600 feet long and at most 200 feet wide, surrounded by deep ravines leading down to the river Seine. On one side a narrow spit of land links the site to its hinterland. A walled town (Les Andelys) stood at the base of the cliff, and Richard

Figure 15. Chateau Gaillard, Les Andelys, France. Richard the Lion Hearted claimed to have built his "cocky castle" on the border of Normandy in only a year, but no one believes he did. The walls, towers, and courtyards of the huge castle cover the narrow hill top, creating a system of barricades known as a defense in depth. An independent fortification at the left blocks access to the main structure, whose great tower still rises above the walls at the right. The area is roughly the size of two modern football fields. *Photograph: Marilyn Stokstad.*

also built a tower on a small island in the river. Dams and obstacles in the water inhibited an enemy's approach from the river, while during peacetime these river defenses enabled the castle's commander to support the garrison by levying tolls on the river traffic (see Chapter 3, Figure 23). Richard also raised money by selling rights of citizenship to residents of the town.

The castle consists of three separate units along the plateau. An attacking army had to approach the castle along this land route, capturing one fortification after another. First, a walled outer bailey, which was built like an independent castle, blocked the approach. Huge round towers defended its curtain wall. From this outer bailey, a bridge with a drawbridge over a very deep moat led to the gate into the middle bailey. Again a curtain wall with one rectangular and three round towers enclosed a large area where Richard built his inner bailey with its tower. This fortress-within-a-fortress became a concentric (double-walled) castle with a wall that resembled a series of round towers. Rising at one side of this "corrugated" wall and commanding the river side of the castle was the great tower. This tower had massive walls about sixteen feet thick and a battered base that made mining virtually impossible. Its massive pointed keel also deflected blows, and inverted buttresses supported a fighting gallery.

As long as Richard was alive to command and reinforce it, the castle stood securely. But Richard died in 1199, and his brother John was not an effective general. Philip Augustus moved to the attack, laying siege to the castle in the summer of 1203. The constable of the castle was Roger de Lacy of Chester, who had sufficient supplies and a large garrison of about 300 men to hold the castle for King John. Roger expected to hold out for as long as a year, while the English king gathered resources to relieve the castle.

The town and the river fort soon surrendered to the French king, and the siege of the castle began in earnest in August. About 1,500 civilians from Les Andeleys fled to the safety of the castle and added to the strain on the provisions. Aware that he probably could starve the castle into submission, Philip built ditches, walls, and timber towers around the castle to prevent supplies from entering. These fortifications were beyond the defenders' arrow range, so they could not destroy or even harass the attackers. With nothing to do but stand guard, the castle garrison undoubtedly suffered from a loss of morale during the long winter.

Two months into the siege, Roger de Lacy realized he could not feed all the people who had taken refuge within the castle walls. He evicted the oldest and weakest who could not help in the defense, and the French army permitted them to leave. But later when de Lacy had to expel the rest of the town, the French closed their lines. When the people tried to return to the castle, they found the gates locked. Trapped between the opposing forces and forced to live in the ravines around the castle walls, they slowly starved.

The final attack on Chateau Gaillard began at the end of February in 1204. First the French had to take the outer bailey. They used stone-throwing machines to keep up a barrage while they filled the castle ditch so that they could haul in a siege tower. But the French troops were so eager to attack that they did not wait for the tower. Instead they used scaling ladders to climb from the bottom of the ditch to the base of the main tower whose foundations they mined, causing the tower to collapse. With the outer walls breached, the garrison had no choice but to withdraw to the middle bailey.

Again a deep ditch prevented further attack. As the French studied the castle walls, one man, named Peter the Snub Nose, saw a weak point and a possible way in. The arrangement of windows high on one wall suggested there might be a chapel and well-appointed living quarters, which would have garderobes. Peter and his friends searched the base of the wall until they found the place where the drain from the garderobes emptied. In a daring sneak attack, the men climbed up the drain and emerged under a large window where they boosted each other into the castle. Once inside they made so much noise that the castle guard thought a large force had entered. The defenders started a fire hoping to burn up the invaders, but the wind shifted carrying the flames back through the building, and the defenders had to retreat to the inner court-yard. Peter and his men escaped the flames and opened the doors for their comrades.

The end was near. The English had about 180 men left. The attackers smelled victory. They brought in a "cat"—a mobile, roofed gallery—for protection and began to mine the gate. The English cut a counter mine and drove the attackers back, but the double mining operation weakened the base of the wall. The French brought in their stone-throwing machines, and the volleys of rocks combined with the weakened foundations caused the wall to collapse. Still the English fought on—with only 36 knights and 120 other men. They moved into the tower, but to no avail. In March 1204, Chateau Gaillard fell to the army of King Philip Augustus, and with the loss of the castle the English lost their claims to Normandy.

The Siege of Rochester

King Richard the Lion Hearted's brother, King John, lost Chateau Gaillard but gained Rochester Castle (see Figure 6). The barons who opposed King John and forced him to sign a charter of rights (Magna Carta) in 1215 had taken control of Rochester Castle. The king laid siege to it. His troops kept up a steady barrage, hurling rocks with their siege machines, but the garrison threw the missiles back from the battlements with such force and accuracy that they killed the royal troops at an alarming rate. The king's men changed tactics and began to mine the curtain wall. The mining proved successful, and the troops rushed through the breach in the wall to engage the garrison in hand-to-hand combat. The outnumbered rebels retreated to the Norman tower. The miners then went to work again and brought down the southwest corner. But the garrison continued to fight, driving back the royal forces time after time. Supplies ran out in the tower, and the starving garrison finally surrendered after a siege lasting nearly three months. The southwest turret was rebuilt as an up-to-date round tower.

NEW DESIGNS: THE TOWERED WALL

Chateau Gaillard had utilized the last of the newly built, huge great towers, and Rochester had depended on its early twelfth-century tower. During the course of the thirteenth century defense shifted to a towered wall, the enceinte or enclosure castle. Two plans emerged: the castle could rely on a series of courtyards, which had to be taken one after another, or on a concentric defense in which a second wall entirely surrounded the inner wall. Plans became more compact, and buildings filled the space around the wall of the inner bailey. Towers were added to the walls, developing a true curtain wall (so called because it "hung" between towers) in which every section could be seen and defended from projecting towers. The towers themselves were rounded into cylindrical or D-shapes so that no flat surface tempted a battering ram, and every surface could be surveyed. Wherever possible, stone replaced wood at the top of the wall. Stone machicolations replaced wooden hoardings.

Chinon

Two castles are associated with both the French and the English—Chinon and Angers. The castle of Chinon stands on a cliff rising above the Vienne River (Figure 16). A Gallo-Roman camp and then a fortress of the counts of Blois once stood on the site. Later the counts of Anjou acquired Chinon, and King Henry II of England (who was also Count of Anjou) built much of the fortress we see today. Henry died at Chinon in 1189, and his son and heir Richard the Lion Hearted also died at Chinon, after the Battle of Chalus. John Lackland, Henry's youngest son, became king (1199–1216). John had abducted the fiancée of the count of La Marches, Isabelle d'Angouleme, and married her at Chinon. Outraged at his conduct, John's French vassals rebelled, giving Philip Augustus an excuse to attack the English. The French took Chinon in 1205, and the treaty signed at Chinon in 1214 confirmed John's losses.

The castle of Chinon, like Chateau Gaillard, depended on defense in depth and the inaccessibility of its magnificent site. Again the castle con-

Figure 16. Chinon and the castle, France. The castle of Chinon, a favorite residence of the English kings who were also counts of Anjou, was built on cliffs above
the River Vienne near its juncture with the Loire. Like Chateau Gaillard, it illustrates the military principle of defense in depth, especially when approached
from the land, the right side in the photograph. *Photograph: Karen Leider.*

sisted of three parts separated by dry moats. Modern reenactors have constructed, and left, a medieval siege machine in the ditch (see Figure 14).
The earliest section of the castle, the stronghold on the promontory commanding the river, dates to the tenth and eleventh centuries. It had six
towers and later a huge round tower—the "Donjon of Coudray"—built
by Philip Augustus. Used as a prison for the Templars when Philip IV
suppressed them in the fourteenth century, the tower still stands. A deep
ditch separates this early castle from the middle castle, the principal residential ward. On the south side looking out over the river valley was
the royal residence. (Chinon gained fame as the meeting place of Charles
VII, who lived there from 1427 to 1450, and Joan of Arc.) Protecting on
the approach from the land side was the forecastle, which has been demolished. The plan of Chinon is typical of castles where the defense consists of a series of independent fortifications and assumes that as one part
fell to attackers, the defenders could retreat to the next section, all the
time hoping for relief from their allies. Chinon also shows the new dis-
position of domestic buildings—hall, kitchens, lodgings—along the outer
walls resulting in a central courtyard.

Figure 17. The Castle of Angers, France. Even when lowered to form bastions for cannon, the towers of the Castle of Angers amaze us with their huge size. The banded appearance of the masonry represents an efficient building technique using bonding and leveling courses of different materials. Developed by Roman and then Byzantine engineers, the technique was adopted by Muslims and Christians and often used for its decorative effect. *Photograph: Marilyn Stokstad.*

Angers

The castle at Angers has a less imposing site but a remarkable surviving towered wall (Figure 17). Angers was originally a Celtic settlement on the border with Brittany and then a Roman town. The counts of Anjou made Angers their capital in the tenth century. In the thirteenth century Anjou became part of France. Blanche of Castile, the mother of King Louis IX and regent until he came of age in 1234, built much of the huge castle we see today (1228–38). The castle stood on a cliff on the left bank overlooking an island and the river Maine (a tributary of the Loire) at the northwest corner of the old town. A suburb arose across the river on the right bank, and a wall reinforced with rounded towers broken by three fortified gates surrounded the entire city. Outside the walls a moat added to the defenses and also separated the castle from the town. The castle had seventeen towers and two towered gatehouses. Inspired by crusader castles and the walls of Constantinople, the masons raised walls and towers that display dark and light banded layers, a late Roman and Byzantine technique. Only one tower, the Mill Tower on the north corner, still has its original height. The moat now combines a deer park with extensive formal gardens. In constant use, the castle was refurbished in 1384 by Duke Louis II of Anjou, and in 1450 and 1465 by Duke Rene of Anjou.

By the end of the fifteenth century the king's constable remodeled the castle into a fortress designed for artillery. The tall towers, which had lost their effectiveness (towers made excellent targets for gunners), were cut down to the height of the curtain walls (about 58–68 feet) and turned into platforms to support cannon. The walls facing the town were thickened to form a wide platform, and casemates (storage rooms within the walls) were added to all the walls and towers. A barbican and an additional rampart and tower suitable for artillery were also added. This new work was finished by 1592. Later used as an army headquarters and a prison, the castle today is a designated historic monument containing gardens, a chapel, and a museum for the fourteenth-century tapestry known as the Angers Apocalypse.

THE MILITARY ORDERS

Constant warfare, especially against the Muslims, gave rise to a new type of military man—one who combined the character and role of both monk and warrior. These knights, organized into military orders, served officially under the Pope but were essentially independent. Their grand master was both an abbot and a general. They lived under a modified Cistercian rule, and they took monastic vows of obedience, poverty, and chastity. As monks, in theory they owned nothing; for example, their horses and armor were loaned to them by the order. In practice they became a wealthy and often arrogant standing army. Having studied Byzantine and Muslim castles and warfare, they built huge castles that changed castle design in Europe.

These military orders were founded to protect the Christian holy places and to help pilgrims going to the Holy Sepulcher in Jerusalem or to other shrines such as the tomb of St. James in Santiago de Compostela. Two major orders were the Hospitalers and the Templars. The Hospitalers (the Brotherhood of the Hospital of St. John in Jerusalem) was founded about 1070 to assist pilgrims. About 1120 they became a military order known as the Knights of St. John. The knights wore a distinctive black cape with a white cross. When Muslim forces finally drove the Christians from the Holy Land in 1191, they moved first to Rhodes, where they remained until 1522, and then to Malta. There they became the Order of Maltese Knights, and their cross with its split and spreading ends is now called the Maltese Cross. The German branch of the Hospitalers, approved by the Pope in 1199 to care for German pilgrims, became the Teutonic Knights. The Teutonic Knights could be recognized by their white cloaks with black crosses. In 1410 the Teutonic Knights established themselves in Prussia.

The Order of the Temple of Jerusalem was founded in 1118 by Hugues de Payens. The Templars became an international order with over 9,000 commanderies and estates and 870 castles. In Palestine alone they built and manned eighteen castles, and they also fought in Spain and Portugal. Eventually they used their wealth to become international bankers. Suppressed in 1312 by the Pope at the instigation of the French king, Philip the Fair, their leaders were executed and their wealth confiscated. Surviving knights joined the Order of St. John or a new order, the Order of Christ founded by King Dinis of Portugal, in 1319/20. Their emblem was an equal-armed red cross with wide terminals, which they wore on a white cape.

In 1160, the Knights of the Order of Christ had built a monastery-fortress at Tomar in Portugal, on the border between Christians and Moors. A huge rotunda—a two-story octagon with encircling passage-way—commemorates the Holy Sepulcher of Jerusalem. When the suppressed Templars moved to Tomar in 1356, they began to build a vast monastery. The addition of a nave in the sixteenth century turned the original Templar chapel into the sanctuary of the church. In the fifteenth century the Knights of Christ experienced a period of unprecedented influence when the king's uncle, Prince Henry the Navigator (1418–60), was their grand master. The prince built two more cloisters at Tomar and building continued in the sixteenth century. Prince Henry used the enormous wealth of the order to finance the expeditions into the Atlantic and along the coast of Africa that eventually led to the explorations that rounded Africa and reached the Indies. Carrying the red cross of the order on their sails, the ships reached the Cape of Good Hope in 1488, India in 1498, and Brazil in 1500. The three ships of Columbus that sailed to America had the cross of the Order of Christ on their sails.

SUGGESTIONS FOR FURTHER READING

King, D. J. Cathcart. *The Castle in England and Wales: An Interpretative History.* London: Croom Helm, 1988.

Thompson, A. Hamilton. *Military Architecture in England During the Middle Ages.* London: Henry Froude, Oxford University Press, 1912.

Toy, Sidney. *A History of Fortification from 3000 B.C. to A.D. 1700.* New York: Macmillan, 1955.

CHAPTER 3

The Castle as Headquarters: The Political and Economic Role of the Castle

Castles were more than military posts; they were the centers of political and economic power. As government headquarters they were built to impress the local population as well as visitors and rivals. While power was spread among great tenants-in-chief in a system of delegated government, castles in each territory were places where local lords collected taxes, settled disputes, and administered justice. As the thirteenth century progressed, local lords lost some of their political power to kings and their ministers. A growing bureaucracy to serve these emerging states required more and different spaces; administrators needed more halls than towers. Consequently, castles remained the headquarters buildings in their districts but internal arrangements changed.

Greater vassals who assisted at court had to be housed in a style appropriate to their rank; consequently, a castle had to be able to accommodate these aristocrats and their retinues. At each level of society from the king to the peers of the realm to the lesser nobility, each family had its household and retainers. The size and magnificence of a lord's retinue, decked out in colorful livery, reinforced his importance and authority. In fact, when the lord was in residence and holding court, the castle might have more inhabitants than the surrounding villages.

Castles continued to be the focus of economic activity as the center of an agricultural domain. Wealth continued to be measured in land and its produce. The only access the lord had to his wealth was to move from one estate to another consuming products from the harvests. Housing and feeding a household including retainers and servants required vasts amount of food and space for food preparation. For most of the year a castle had only a skeleton staff, the castellan, his family, civil servants, and a few permanent guards. The arrival of the lord meant a massive influx of people and turned a sleepy community into a hub of activity.

A sharp contrast existed between the upper classes who constantly moved from manor to manor and the peasants who were tied to the land and lived in agricultural villages outside the castle walls. Yet economic opportunities expanded for both groups. Both the nobility who wanted more profits and the peasants who wanted more land cut down the forests, drained the swamps, and turned them into productive land. As labor and produce were converted to money, nobles became landlords and moved into the emerging cities, leaving a constable in charge of the castle and tenants on the land. Farmers produced enough food to support cities as well as villages; however, large cities remained vulnerable to famine caused by wars and poor harvests.

The Black Death in the fourteenth century reduced the population and gave workers the upper hand. By the end of the Middle Ages economic power had shifted to the cities, and rich peasants had bought their land. These people formed a new prosperous class; however, life still had many risks, and changes in status could move up or down from generation to generation (Documents 57–60).

HEADQUARTERS CASTLES

What did these headquarters castles look like? The builders of castles began to emphasize curtain walls and towers rather than a single great tower, and so the castle became an "enclosure" castle or enceinte. The garrison had more space, so the castle could assume a greater role in the offense. For example, during sieges the garrison used their own hurling machines to fire missiles back at the attackers. When the terrain permitted, rectangular ground plans replaced the irregular plans of the twelfth-century castles. Walls became higher and thicker, and the masonry spread outward at the bottom to form a sloping "talus" that prevented the effective use of battering rams or mining. At the top of the wall, stone machicolations replaced wooden hoardings, and tile roofs might even cover the wall-walks. Wall and corner towers became independent strongholds although some were built as half cylinders with an open back to prevent an enemy from using a captured tower against the garrison. The top of the tower might be flat and used as a firing platform, or it might be covered with a conical roof (compare Figures 11 and 17). Sometimes, to save costly materials and the builders' time, turrets known as "pepper pots" replaced towers on the upper wall. Around the castle, doubled encircling walls created open spaces known as lists (see Figure 13). Lists made convenient places for the garrison to exercise and train and for archers to practice (Document 63). In times of peace the knights held mock battles, or tournaments, in the lists, and townspeople held markets and fairs. In wartime the garrison set up their stone-throwing machines, and peasants and townspeople took refuge in the lists.

The castle had to accommodate several functions within its walls: a magnificent great hall with ample space to hold court and serve state banquets (as well as impress and intimidate visitors); huge barns to store grain; stables and shelters for animals; lodging for workers; and all manner of workshops. The heavily fortified and residential gatehouse, where the governor of the castle could live and also direct an active defense of his castle, replaced the single great tower. Nevertheless, the great tower survived as a symbol of power, as seen at the Earl Marshall's castle of Pembroke in Wales (see Figure 3) or the French royal castle of the Louvre in Paris.

The Louvre

Between 1180 and 1220 the French king Philip Augustus built the castle of the Louvre as part of a massive city wall. (Parts of the wall can still be seen in the Marais district behind the Hotel de Sens and near the Church of St.-Etienne-du-Monte.) The castle of the Louvre was a secure place to house the royal treasure and archives. The great tower—a round central tower—was over one hundred feet high and sixty feet in diameter, with walls twelve to thirteen feet thick. (Today the base of the tower forms part of the underground entrance to the Louvre Museum.) The tower stood in a rectangular court, surrounded by curtain walls with corner towers. Towered gates opened in the center of the south and east walls. In the fourteenth century Charles V added more residential accommodations, and in 1527 Francis I destroyed the medieval towers and walls to build a Renaissance royal palace and gardens.

Royal Palace on the Ile de la Cité

On the Ile de la Cité, the island in the Seine at the heart of Paris, the principal royal palace and the administrative center of the growing French kingdom was built west of the cathedral of Notre Dame. A residence had stood on the site since Merovingian times, giving the site an aura of antiquity and established power. The palace as it evolved was not one but several buildings, including a twelfth-century great tower (today the Tour Bonbec) and chamber block, the thirteenth-century chapel (the Ste.-Chapelle), a merchants' hall, and a hall attached to the tower overlooking the river (the Salle sur l'Eau) built by Louis IX. In the 1290s, Philip IV added more specialized government buildings—a royal audience hall and hall of justice (the Grand Salle). In the great hall the king held court, received guests and petitioners, and held state receptions and banquets. He and his advisers administered justice, so the building also had to function as a courthouse and prison. Of course, the royal residence and gardens were luxurious. The castle reflected a social system that continued even as the actual forms of government—and power—changed. The Knights' Hall at Mont St.-Michel, even without tapestries on the walls and benches near the fireplaces, helps us imagine the appearance of the royal halls of Paris (Figure 18).

THE CASTLE AS SEAT OF GOVERNMENT

In the last decades of the thirteenth century the great age of the feudal castle was coming to an end. Led by the kings of France and England, rulers consolidated their power and created national states permitting only royal castles, or castles in the hands of loyal followers. Furthermore, castles had become so large and expensive to build and maintain that they required the vast resources of an entire kingdom. Builder monarchs beggared their kingdoms as they poured money into castles and churches.

As a secure residence for its owner, the castle established a natural center for the king's or lord's exercise of power. In the case of minor lords the power was local, but for the king and his deputies, the castle could become a true seat of government, in effect a capital. The castle with its massive towers was an appropriate and reasonable place to store valuable

Figure 18. The Knights' Hall (scriptorium); Mont St.-Michel, France. The work-room, or scriptorium, where books were copied and illuminated, in the monastery of Mont St.-Michel was built in the first decades of the thirteenth century. The room suggests the appearance of the great halls once found in castles and palaces. Columns with carved capitals support a ribbed groined vault and divide the space into bays. Tapestries could be hung to form semiprivate compartments. Large windows and fireplaces provided light and heat, and two guarderobes were additional amenities. *Gramstorff Collection, Photographic Archives, National Gallery of Art, Washington, DC.*

insignia that served as proof of power, as well as records and documents such as charters, expense rolls, and accounts to meet the legal and financial needs of the government in an increasingly literate (and litigious) age.

Paris

In Paris the king's hall, rebuilt after a fire, served as the great hall for parliament, complete with guard room and a kitchen that could feed two thousand people. The building also included the treasury and business offices for tax and financial affairs. Philip IV remodeled the older buildings on the Ile de la Cité, beginning about 1290 by joining them with corridors and surrounding the complex with walls and towers.

As it finally emerged in the fourteenth century, the architecture of the king's residence imposed an orderly progression from public to increasingly secure and isolated space. The visitor (or petitioner) moved through the main gate into a large courtyard with the chapel at the left and great hall to the right and climbed a magnificent stairway to the merchants' gallery, turning right to enter the audience hall (hall of justice) which led to the council chamber. If one turned neither left nor right but moved straight ahead, one arrived at the royal apartments and the garden, the most private space of all. The isolation of the royal person made that person seem important and sought after, but public display was an essential part of government. On special occasions, when the king met the public, the merchants would clear their hall and people could move directly through the building. The show of authority and the symbols of power could be as important as power itself.

Caernarfon

The castles of Wales are among the best examples of a medieval governmental military complex. In Wales the English kings Henry III (1216–72) and Edward I (1272–1307) constructed a group of castles for both military and administrative use, determined as they were to hold the rebellious territory. Edward I planned a series of castles across northern Wales—Conway (1283–87), Caernarfon (1283/5–1322/3), Harlech (1285–90), and Beaumaris (1295–1320)—all designed by James of St. George (1235–1305). Caernarfon had ample space for nonmilitary functions. It housed the court of law, the state records and archives, and the treasury. It was also what scholars today call an "elite residence" and a bastide; that is, it was a fortified palace and had an attached fortified town. The castle and city at Caernarfon became the de facto English capital of Wales, and even today the heir to the British throne is invested as Prince of Wales at Caernarfon.

Edward had seen the Muslim and Christian castles while on crusade in 1270, and he recognized the value of their emphasis on walls rather than a single tower. He returned home by way of Savoy. To build Caernarfon, Edward brought from Savoy a military engineer and archi-

Figure 19. Gatehouse and lower court, Castle of Caernarfon, Wales. Built at the end of the thirteenth century, Caernarfon was the English king's governmental center in northern Wales. At the far right of the photograph is the King's Gate, the most complex gate built in medieval England and Wales. The lower court-yard contained the residence of the governor, a residence for the queen, and the great hall and the kitchens. The castle was accessible from the water and two watergates opened into this lower court. *Photograph: Karen Leider.*

tect, James of St. George (c. 1235–1305), who took charge of the design and building of the king's proposed chain of castles.

For his principal castle in Wales, Edward chose a site dominating the Menai Strait, the ancient Roman settlement of Segontium where an eleventh-century motte and bailey castle had already been built by Hugh of Avranche, Earl of Chester. The castle as we see it today was built between 1283 and 1323 and never finished (Figure 19).

Caernarfon has an exceptionally fine plan, with upper and lower wards (courtyards) forming an hourglass shape. The curtain wall stretches between thirteen towers—two flanking the King's Gate, two flanking the Queen's Gate, seven huge polygonal towers, one small cistern tower, and a small watch tower. Complex battlements included a crenellated wall-walk and towers and double shooting galleries, one above the other. When hoardings were added during wartime, three rows of archers could defend the same section of wall. Rather than simple arrow loops, triple radiating embrasures with single outside arrow slits pierced the wall, allowing many archers to shoot simultaneously. All the towers are independent barriers, separating segments of the wall from each other; consequently, if an enemy gained the top of the wall, he could not move easily to another section.

The castle had two principal entrances. The King's Gate, or main entrance from town, was an elaborate two-tower gatehouse. A drawbridge over a moat on the town side (today a modern bridge) led to a complex entry that was planned to include a series of five heavy doors and six portcullises, ending in a second drawbridge. The second story provided space for guard rooms, the operation of the portcullises and drawbridges, and even the castle's chapel. Never finished, the gatehouse was intended to extend across the castle from wall to wall, dividing the space into upper and lower wards.

Master James of St. George incorporated the Norman mound into the upper yard as the site of the Queen's Gate (the southeast gate). Consequently the Queen's Gate opens high above the town, protected by towers and machicolations. A long ramp with a turning bridge rather than a drawbridge once linked the gate to the land below. Remains of bridge works are still visible, but the ramp may never have been finished.

The governor (justiciar) of Wales lived in the powerful Eagle Tower in the lower court at the western end of the castle. From the top of this huge polygonal tower three turrets or watch towers overlook the Menai Strait and command the approaches to the castle. Each turret was decorated with the sculpture of an eagle, the coat of arms of the first governor Sir Otto de Grandson. The tower had a basement and three stories, each with a large central room and chambers in the walls. The chambers housed a chapel, a kitchen, and garderobes. On the ground floor, a watergate with a portcullis opened to the Menai Strait. Distinguished visitors arriving by boat entered the castle here.

In the Well Tower next to the King's Gate, another watergate permitted easy access to deliver supplies to the kitchens. The kitchens were of timber and filled the space along the wall between the towers. The great hall also stood in the lower court, across from the kitchens and next to the Queen's Tower. Only the foundations survive to give us an idea of sizes. All the rooms were spacious and well lit, and equipped with fireplaces and garderobes. The names of the towers—the Chamberlain's or

Record Tower and the Queen's Tower—recall the castle's use as both an administrative center and a residence.

In Wales the contrast between the great cylindrical tower at Pembroke (see Figure 3) and the towered walls of Caernarfon highlight the shifting political and economic expectations. Sieges such as that of Chateau Gaillard had pointed out the weakness of military tactics based on a gradual retreat to an isolated tower. The future clearly lay with reinforced walls. A large open space inside the walls allowed a larger number of men to move rapidly from place to place, defending the walls and using wall towers and sally ports to mount surprise attacks.

The strength of the permanent garrison at Caernarfon is known from the accounts kept during Edward I's reign. The constable was in charge of the castle, assisted by two "Serjeant horsemen." In addition there were ten crossbowmen, a smith, a carpenter, a "mechanic," and twenty-five footmen at arms, for a total of forty men. At the beginning of the fifteenth century the castle was staffed by a hundred professional soldiers—twenty men-at-arms and eighty archers. At the same time the castle at Harlech had ten men-at-arms and thirty archers. (This information and more can be found in A *History of Fortification* by Sidney Toy, New York: Macmillan, 1955, pp. 210–11, quoting Welsh Roll Chancery, 12 Edw. I, 1284, Memb. 5; cat. Rot. Wall., 288, and Acts of the Privy Council, Vol. II, Henry IV, pp. 64–66.)

Harlech

Caernarfon with its asymmetrically positioned towers and irregular plan suggests the traditional castle design, which reflects the topography. But James of St. George also developed a new concentric castle plan, which had double encircling walls and an overall symmetrical, rectangular plan. Harlech brilliantly demonstrates the geometric perfection desired by Master James. Lower outer walls and higher inner walls form a square within a square, and towers rise above towers. The castle had an open inner court with the massive defenses focused on the main gate, which became the residence of the governor of the castle. A large square building with corner towers and a pair of towers that flank the portal, the gatehouse expanded from a place for guards and portcullis machinery to a full hall with private rooms, facing both the inner court and out to the country or city.

Figure 20. Harlech Castle, Wales. This early photograph shows the castle before modern restoration and encroaching buildings. A fortress gatehouse (upper right), curtain walls, and corner tower plus the remarkable site enabled the castle garrison to withstand sieges until they were starved into submission. The sea once came up to the base of the cliff; the flat land at the left and the area occupied by the road and houses would have been under water. *Gramstorff Collection, Photographic Archives, National Gallery of Art, Washington, DC.*

High above the bay (which is now silted in) on a sheer cliff 200 feet high, the castle at Harlech covers a small plateau (Figure 20). To enter the castle the visitor had to pass through a barbican, cross over a causeway that spanned a forty-foot-wide ditch, pass through the outer gate, and only then arrive at the gatehouse, which had strong doors and portcullises. The gatehouse at Harlech covers an area of eighty feet by fifty-four feet, and has three stories with an inner tower, which can be cut off from the rest of the castle. Across the inner ward from the gatehouse stands the great hall, its windows looking out to the sea. Kitchens and buttery were at one side; the chapel, work rooms, storage rooms, and well on the other. Walls down the cliff link the castle to a watergate that can be reached by narrow steps and walk which are barred by a gate and drawbridge. The defensive system proved itself during sieges in 1404, 1408–9, and 1451–68. In the last siege, the castle garrison was starved into surrender, their heroism commemorated in the Welsh anthem, "Men of Harlech."

Fourteenth-Century Changes

Change came to architecture as well as other facets of life in the four-teenth century with the spread of disease, famine, and war. The bubonic plague, called the Black Death, began in 1348 and recurred in following years. Although figures are uncertain, the plagues may have killed a third of Europe's population in some places. Entire villages disappeared. To add to the misery of the people, France and England engaged in the futile, drawn-out Hundred Years War from 1337 to 1453. Castles were built, de-stroyed, and rebuilt, but villages and peasants' fields and orchards were also destroyed (Document 59). Architects and patrons turned to small projects rather than the grand designs of the thirteenth century. Often the builders reverted to the twelfth-century tower, now referred to as a "tower house" to distinguish it from the earlier "great tower." The build-ing was usually a rectangular block with corner turrets.

Improvements continued to be made in the details of castle design, for example, in the operation of portcullises and drawbridges and in the use of barbicans. For those who could afford them, moats and stone machico-lations became an even more important part of the defensive scheme. Wall-walks and towers might be expanded with a double set of machico-lations. Since machicolations were very expensive, however, they might be built only above the door, like a balcony. Such a feature is called a brattice. As artillery came into general use, elaborate wall tops became less important; in fact, battlements were easily destroyed by the gunners. Cannons and guns were used in Italy in 1304 and 1315, in Rouen in 1338, and at the Battle of Crecy on the August 26, 1346. Crenellated and machicolated walls and towers continued to be built as decorative elements, symbols for a castle rather than functional military elements.

The castle's residential aspects also changed in the fourteenth century as people demanded more comfortable living conditions. Owners added domestic wings to halls and filled the castle's courtyard with multistoried buildings as well as service quarters. Eventually structures built along the walls reduced the bailey into an inner courtyard. In fine houses large win-dows filled with elegant tracery and glass replaced some of the wooden shutters and made great halls both pleasant and splendid. Sculptured coats of arms over portals and fireplaces proclaimed the family's heritage. In short, private castles became palaces.

As more emphasis was placed on domestic requirements, moats could be defensive (Document 52) and at the same time ponds for raising frogs and fish. The castle might have a dovecote, the birds providing meat and eggs to eat, and a roost for the trained homing pigeons that provided a rapid messenger service. Many a castle was surrounded by a hunting park since hunting was a popular noble exercise and recreation. The deer, boar, and small game could also be a source of meat and fur. A chapel in the castle provided for spiritual needs of the residents, and the castle might be associated with a parish church or monastery, formed by and dependent on the lord of the castle.

The castle and church formed the core of a village (Document 53). As the center of the king's or the lord's desmene, the castle normally controlled important public facilities, such as the mill. A mill was essential for both the castle household and the people of the village. Without a mill the bakers could not produce the bread that was the mainstay of the diet—it took an enormous amount of bread to support a household. The mill and ovens provided a handsome income for their owners.

The Manor House

Lesser landholders seldom had the resources or the need to build castles, but they often had to fortify their homes (Document 54). The manor house was the local economic, residential, and administrative center and might be given the honorific title of "castle." Stokesay Castle is a well-preserved example of the fortified manor house (Figure 21). Today, in a reversal of the usual castle ruins where we find outer walls but an empty bailey, the inner buildings still stand at Stokesay while the defensive walls are gone and the moat is dry. An Elizabethan gatehouse has replaced the original entryway. Laurence of Ludlow inherited the manor, and acquired a "license to crenellate" from Edward I in 1290. He added a curtain wall, moat, and a tower with a turret at each end of an already existing hall. The hall has large windows and a chamber at each end.

Another kind of defensible country home characterizes Scotland and other border regions (see Figure 30). Beginning in the fourteenth century, local lords on both sides of the English Scottish borders built residential towers set in a walled yard called a barmkyn. The buildings are rectangular or Z-shaped in plan, and have three or four stories joined by

Figure 21. Fortified manor house, Stokesay, England. Usually castle walls stand and the interior buildings have been destroyed. At Stokesay, the walls are gone and the manor house with its well-lit hall, massive tower at the right, and timbered private rooms at the left remain. *Photograph: Marilyn Stokstad.*

a spiral staircase. The top of the tower was crowned by battlements and turrets. Like the Norman tower, these tower houses used the first floor for storage and had their principal hall on the second or even the third floor. The hall was the seat of local justice. One or two projecting wings might be built to add additional space for living rooms, giving the tower a distinctive Z-shaped plan. Larger windows, fireplaces, and garderobes were added to rooms on third and fourth levels. The top of the building could be quite elaborate and have two levels of battlements, with machicolations and turrets corbelled out over the walls. The door was protected by an iron grille called a yet. These tower houses were still being built in the seventeenth century.

THE FORTIFIED CITY

While not strictly castles, fortified towns gained in importance and until they approached the strength—and appearance—of castles. Some towns that grew up near monasteries or castles, at trade and transportation centers, required increasingly sophisticated defenses. At first, low walls and gates distinguished a town with its royal privileges from the countryside, which lay under the control of the local lord. Town gates, locked at night, kept out strangers. By the thirteenth and fourteenth centuries a town like Carcassonne in southern France had walls, towers, and battlements that could rival a castle (see Figures 11–13).

Within the city walls, people with the same interests and occupations lived together in small districts. Twisting streets and alleys led to a few public squares. Sanitation was minimal and depended on rain. Public services and safety were nonexistent. Tradespeople combined workshop, sales room, and living quarters in a single building that stood three or four stories high with brick or timber walls and thatched roofs. Fire was a constant hazard. In short, life was hard and dangerous but stimulating (Document 60). The energetic and creative people found their way to the towns and cities, leaving the more conservative to live as peasants working the land and living in feudal villages.

Carcassonne

Carcassonne was an important military and commercial center in southern France. A key stronghold since Roman times and the capital of a county by the ninth century, Carcassonne was as much a military center as any castle. Having survived many sieges, it was abandoned in 1240 and rebuilt by Louis IX in 1248. The city has double curtain walls; the outer has twenty towers and the inner, twenty-five (see Figure 13). Some of the towers are independent fortresses and even have their own wells. A barbican and complex outerworks guard the main city gate. The architect Viollet-le-Duc restored the medieval city in the nineteenth century, adding conical tiled roofs inappropriate to southern French architecture. The citadel is rectangular in plan, with rooms and towers arranged around an open central courtyard. A deep moat cuts the citadel off from the city.

The Bastide of Aigues Mortes

New towns established by royal decree in the thirteenth century for military purposes are called bastides. In France, bastides were laid out like

Figure 22. City walls, Aigues Mortes, France. Founded as a port for crusaders in the thirteenth century, the city has relatively low walls and many gates that once provided an easy access to the ships. The top of the wall has a wide walk and crenellations tall enough to protect the guards. To prevent treasonable tunneling, no houses were permitted next to the walls. This space also enabled soldiers to move rapidly into defensive positions. The tower at the left is one of the fortified gates. *Photograph: Marilyn Stokstad.*

ancient Roman cities, with a rectangular plan and two principal streets crossing at right angles, dividing the city into four sections with the market square and the church at the center. Walls with towers and fortified gates surrounded the bastide. As duke of Aquitaine, Edward I of England established over fifty bastides as administrative headquarters and commercial centers. These towns were fortified only lightly.

The city or bastide of Aigues Mortes was established on the Mediterranean coast by Louis IX as the embarkation spot for his crusade (Figure 22). Rectangular in plan with streets parallel to the walls, and a central open square, five gates on the sea side served the port. The walls were about thirty-five feet high with both wall and corner towers. The Tour de Constance, finished in 1248, a round, moated independent tower, over 100 feet tall with walls nearly 20 feet thick, provided extra security for the governor. The tall turret rising above the wall-walk served as both a watch tower and a lighthouse. Inside the walls, the streets ran straight from gate to gate, crossing at right angles to form rectangular blocks of buildings. A central town square and church served the community's spiritual and social-commercial needs. Building stopped around 1300. Today the harbor is silted up, and Aigues-Mortes survives as a well-preserved relic of the past.

The Citadel

A fortress or citadel (Italian: *cittadella*, small city) might be built as part of the city defenses. Edward I's castle at Caernarfon in Wales and the palace of the counts at Carcassonne combine citadels and bastides. A citadel usually had gates leading both into the city through the city wall and out to the countryside. The citadel was designed like a castle and staffed and supplied to withstand a siege. It served as an army headquarters and supply depot, and it provided a last line of defense for the residents of the town. The citadel also played a symbolic role, since it expressed the authority of its lord—the king, duke, or bishop, or their representatives—and also established the importance of the city. As an aristocratic residence, the citadel could be a luxurious palace. As a fortress, it controlled the population through its expression of awesome might in towers and walls. Since the citadel was the governmental center, it was associated with tax collection and possibly the residence of an arrogant garrison, which made the citadel and its residents the frequent focus of town ire. Rebellions centered on the citadel, and independent citizens tried to either tear them down or staff them with their own men.

Castle of Saint Antoine

A new kind of castle appeared in France as part of the city defenses. The barbican of the gate became a large independent castle known as a bastille. As military architecture, the bastille was a new form, also called a "block castle," in which the eight towers and walls of a rectangular building were the same height and created a large terrace that could be used as a firing platform. The Castle of Saint Antoine at the northeast entrance to Paris, built between 1370 and 1382, became the infamous Bastille prison destroyed by the people in 1789 at the beginning of the French revolution.

EMERGING COMMERCIAL CENTERS

In Germany and Italy central authority was unknown, and local lords in Germany and independent cities in Italy built defensive works. By the end of the eleventh century in Italy, townspeople in Venice, Milan, and Lucca sought the king's protection from feudal lords. The kings soon realized that using the city money enabled them to become independent of their nobility by hiring mercenary troops. Italian cities were among the largest and most prosperous in Europe.

Castles of the Rhine

Political and economic powers unite in the Rhine River valley where castles controlled river traffic and served as toll stations. Individual lords could become piratical in their collection practices. Along the Rhine and Danube local authorities controlled travel, collecting endless toll from castles seemingly on every hilltop. Not far from the famous Lorelei Rock (according to local legend, the home of a nymph whose songs lured boatmen to death in the rapids) are the castle of Gutenfels, the village of Kaub, and toll fortress the Pfalz (Figure 23).

Gutenfels

The castle of Gutenfels is a typical German thirteenth to fourteenth-century mountain castle with a tall tower, a fortified and crenellated dwelling, and a walled courtyard. According to legend it was named for the Lady Guta, the sister of the Count of Kaub who married Richard of Cornwall after he won her by fighting in a tournament in Cologne. After surviving centuries of sieges and rebuilding, the castle was nearly lost in 1805–7 when Napoleon ordered its destruction. The castle was dismantled and everything of value was taken and sold. The castle became one of the many romantic ruins on the Rhine. Then, Gutenfels came into the possession of the Cologne architect Gustav Walter, who rebuilt it as his own home in 1889–92. He created his own romantic vision of a medieval castle complete with knights' hall and fighting galleries, but he also added bathrooms with hot and cold running water. Today, the castle is a restaurant and hotel.

Figure 23. Kaub with Pfalz and Gutenfels castles, Germany. This early photo, taken before modern buildings and restorations intrude, illustrates the relationship of the castle on the hill, the town by the Rhine River, and the toll castle on the rock in the middle of the river. *Gramstorff Collection, Photographic Archives, National Gallery of Art, Washington, DC.*

The Village of Kaub and the Pfalz

At the foot of the mountain, beside the river, the village of Kaub was once the toll collection point and a river pilot station. Today it is a picturesque wine town. The most distinctive building of this complex is the Pfalzgrafenstein (usually shortened to "the Pfalz"). In 1326–27 Ludwig of Bavaria built a small fortress on a rock in midstream in order to control shipping on the river and also to help break up the winter ice. At first the river castle consisted of a five-sided tower six stories high. In 1338–42 a six-sided turreted outer wall was added. (The curving roof is a Baroque addition.) The castle continued in government use into the nineteenth century and still works as a breakwater. Since it can be reached only by boat, it never became a restaurant—the fate of many German castles—and in 1967–75 it was restored to its original brilliant white plaster and red stained wood. The castles of the Rhine helped inspire the romantic revival and the creation of a German identity in the nineteenth and twentieth centuries. Today they are an important part of Germany's tourist industry.

SUGGESTIONS FOR FURTHER READING

Coulson, Charles L. *Castles in Medieval Society, Fortresses in England, France and Ireland in the Central Middle Ages*. Oxford: Oxford University Press, 2003.

Emery, Anthon. *Greater Medieval Houses of England and Wales, 1300–1500*. Cambridge, UK: Cambridge University Press, 1996. (Volumes 1 and 2.)

Johnson, Matthew. *Behind the Castle Gate: From Medieval to Renaissance*. London and New York: Routledge, 2002.

Taylor, Robert R. *The Castles of the Rhine, Recreating the Middle Ages in Modern Germany*. Waterloo, Ontario: Wilfrid Laurier University Press, 1998.

THE CASTLE AS SYMBOL AND PALACE

Whether looming over the land as a symbol of a ruler's authority or providing a setting for displays of wealth and power in spectacular feasts and tournaments, castles made a visual statement about their owners. All architecture has symbolic overtones, and the castle is a potent image.

In the eleventh and twelfth centuries, mounds, palisades, and ditches were enough to indicate a seat of power, but as stone masonry replaced timber, towers and crenellated palisades and rooflines defined the castle. The licenses to crenellate, which the king issued as official permission to fortify a place or residence, indicated a social status as much as a need for defense. In the fourteenth century, the introduction of gunpowder in wars irrevocably changed the nature of battles and affected the design of castles. High walls and tall towers made excellent targets, so builders emphasized defense in depth—low walls and wide moats. Eventually earlier castles became an encumbrance because maintenance of a huge masonry structure drained resources better spent on men and munitions. Nevertheless, the idea of a castle—the castle as a symbol—lived on.

As warfare changed, the king needed money to pay armies of mercenary troops, but as we have seen the oldest and most distinguished nobles counted their wealth in land, not money. Newly rich city people who engaged in commerce had the necessary ready cash. Consequently the king and a few forward-looking nobles favored the cities. They founded new cities and gave the burghers positions at court. These retainers, who wanted to be associated with power and prestige, formed a new social hierarchy. An important way for one of these "new men" to establish himself in the eyes of his neighbors was to build a splendid castle for his family home. Meanwhile those already in the feudal hierarchy crenel-

Figure 24. Leeds Castle, England. The park-like setting belies the efficiency of water barriers in castle design, but castle designers were also aware of the impressive effect they could create. *Photograph: Karen Leider.*

lated and refurbished their inherited castles. The addition of crenellated battlements to a simple domestic building gave it and the owner immediate stature and credibility. Even today, we can still see crenellations decorating college halls, government buildings, and even private houses.

Just as towers and crenellations indicated a building's status, so the crenellated wall signified a castle in the visual arts and in that distinctive medieval sign language known as heraldry. The heraldic symbol of the kingdom of Castile, for example, consisted of a wall and three crenellated towers. This simple composition was easily recognized and reproduced. As the emblem of the powerful French queen Blanche of Castile (the mother of Louis IX and regent during his childhood, 1226–34) the heraldic castle appears beside the lilies of France in works of art, such as the stained glass windows of the cathedral of Chartres and the Ste.-Chapelle in Paris.

SYMBOLIC ARCHITECTURE

Castles were designed to intimidate, or at least impress, visitors (Figures 24 and 25). Any castle reinforced the impression of overwhelming power and the authority of its owner or his constable (castellan or governor of the castle). In an age of personal government, the architectural

Figure 25. Grand stair, Bishop's Palace, St. David's, Wales. Few of the grand palatial stairways still exist, but the Bishop's Palace boasts of two. The normal medieval stairway was an unimpressive and often difficult tight spiral fit into the wall of the building. *Photograph: Karen Leider.*

design of the castle played an important role in the control of the access to the lord and so to power. The increasing complexity of the physical relationship of the hall of justice, the presence chamber, and the private rooms of the lord may have been accidental or calculated but certainly had an effect. The guest or petitioner moved from public to increasingly private space, through corridors, courts with views, waiting rooms, and gates—until the lord is revealed in the great hall seated in a splendid chair on a raised dais. The castle plan was intended to be spatially confusing, both for protection and also to enhance the position of power through the difficulty of access. In time, however, the individual halls became a continuous series of rooms built against the walls and having the appearance and effect of a single building with an inner courtyard.

Matthew Johnson imagines and describes the typical visitor's arrival at the castle in his book, *Behind the Castle Gate*. At first sight the castle, whether emerging from the woods of a hunting park or rising in the distance on a hill, created an expectation of grandeur within. Arriving at the gate at last, the visitor waiting to be admitted had time to study the symbolic heraldic imagery decorating the gatehouse or towers. Coats of arms established the lineage and family connections of the lord of the castle. Even the form of admission into the castle depended on one's place in the social hierarchy. Trumpeters on the walls might greet important visitors who then entered through wide open doors. Lesser people entered quietly through a small door called the wicket, cut into the main door. A wicket gate sometimes even required the visitor to bend over in order to enter. The least important people might be sent around to the postern, which became a back door, not a hidden sally port.

The Gatehouse

A massive gatehouse provided an intricate defense with its portcullis, arrow slits, and murder holes, but it also could make the guest feel vulnerable. This intimidating tunnel-like entrance opened suddenly into a spacious bailey or courtyard. The visiting knight dismounted and left his horse in the lower court near the door, then walked the rest of the way, across the open space. Since a knight was defined by the quality of his horses and armor, and his horse was his own symbol of power, to leave his mount and proceed on foot established his peaceful intent and the superior importance of the lord of the castle. Once through the lower courtyard and into the upper, the visitor finally saw the castle's principal residential building—the center of power, the great hall.

The Great Hall

From the great hall the lord and his family could observe everything going on in the courtyard from large windows lighting the ceremonial end of the room. The hall itself might have sculptural decoration around the entrance and windows, which through its symbolism told of the family's lineage and importance. The visitor approaching the hall knew that he was very much on view and might identify himself by wearing distinctive colors or clothing embroidered with his heraldic coat of arms. Once the visitor crossed the open space and reached the hall, he might have to climb a staircase, although perhaps not as impressive as the bishop's at St. David's (see Figure 25) and perhaps enter through a porch before proceeding through corridors and perhaps a small waiting chamber into the lower end of the hall. A typical great hall was a single rectangular room with a raised dais with high table and/or throne at one end and a wooden screen at the other, which separated the hall from the service rooms and also shielded those within from drafts. The main door opened into this screens passage. The visitor had to walk the length of the hall, facing the lord enthroned on the dais, and once arriving, he was expected to kneel or bow.

The hall was the center of life in the castle. In early times everyone lived and ate together there. The hall became the judicial and ceremonial center of the castle—the center of feudal power, homage, and exchange of gifts. As time passed the lord, his family, and confidants withdrew from this fellowship to private chambers; nevertheless, the lord ceremonially ate with his people at regular intervals. Feasting was a social act, reinforcing the bonds of community and mutual support and trust. The arrangement of the tables in the hall is still followed at many formal dinners today. The head table for important people is placed at one end of the room and the rest of the tables are perpendicular to it. In the medieval hall large windows lit the head table. Window seats created small private rooms within the thickness of the wall. Originally a central hearth warmed the people in the hall, but wall fireplaces and chimneys came into use by the twelfth century.

Domestic Quarters

The family departed from the hall by going through doors at the upper end to the private residential part of the building. A corridor and a waiting room that might have a fireplace and even a garderobe led to the lord's chamber, where business and political discussions took place under the watchful eyes of other retainers. The chamber often looked out over

a garden, and from this garden the lord's "closet" with archives and treasury could be reached. The ladies had separate suites with an enclosed garden and sometimes a private chapel, all linked by covered walks. Farther
removed from the hall were lodgings for important guests.

Visitors were usually known at least by reputation to the castle residents. At no time was the elite class very large. Matthew Johnson notes
in *Behind the Castle Gate* that in England in 1436 the tax returns indicate that there were only 51 peers, 183 greater knights, and 750 lesser
knights. Even when one considers the wives and children of these 984
men, only a small number of people belonged to this class (Matthew
Johnson, *Behind the Castle Gate*, p. 63). Not only did these people know
each other, they were also often related through marriage. Royal or baronial, lord or vassal—each had his household, consisting of family, retainers, and servants. Only the scale differed. An important medieval
household might have as many as 2,000 people. The castle provided the
architectural setting, accommodating people and their activities in a
great hall and supported by kitchens and storerooms and a secure strong
room for archives and treasure.

The Castle Transformed

In the later years of the fourteenth century the desire for spacious,
comfortable living arrangements surpassed the need for defensive outer
walls. The hall remained the center of the residential complex. Large
windows filled with elegant tracery and glass and protected by wooden
shutters made great halls both pleasant and splendid. Sculpture on portals and fireplaces proclaimed the family's heritage. Used for great occasions and feasts during most of the year, the hall was simply a large
enclosed space, and as such it could shelter servants and travelers. The
owner lived in a suite of private rooms—a solar or smaller hall, having
retiring rooms, library, and office or study. Every great house also had its
chapel and rooms for the chaplain. Other support areas included the
kitchen, buttery, and pantry. They were still linked to the hall and to
suites of rooms in the traditional arrangement. Most rooms had fireplaces,
and garderobes adjoined every suite of rooms.

When times were peaceful and land available, suites of rooms spread
out around a quadrangle. Often domestic wings were added to older
buildings. Halls and multistoried houses built along the castle walls filled

the inner yard until what had been a multipurpose space became the inner court of a palace. In unstable areas such as the Scottish Borders and the Italian cities, tower houses were the norm. In tower houses the rooms were stacked instead of placed side by side.

The stone walls we see today give a false idea of the castle interior. People in the Middle Ages loved brilliant colors. Aristocrats and royals spent enormous sums on tapestries, the woven wall hangings that turned the bare walls and drafty rooms into rich and colorful displays of educational and moral messages—historical and literary themes, religious subjects, and heraldry. Since a powerful lord had many manors where he had to reside in order to use the produce paid as tax and to administer the estate, the tapestries could be packed in trunks and carried from place to place as their owners moved. Furniture was highly functional—wooden tables, stools, beds—and was also covered with woven and embroidered textiles. Clothing was just as rich and colorful.

Bodiam Castle

Bodiam Castle in Sussex demonstrates Matthew Johnson's point that social and symbolic messages sent out by the castle architecture became more meaningful than the military function (Figure 26). Johnson provides a close analysis of its design. Sir Edward Dallyngrigge (or Dallingridge; spellings were not fixed in those days) built this castle after retiring from almost thirty years of military service. As a younger son, he could not inherit the family estate, but during the Hundred Years War soldiers like Sir Edward could make a fortune from booty and ransom. When he settled down, Sir Edward married an heiress who also contributed her dowry to the building program. In October 1385 Sir Edward obtained a "license to crenellate," and for the next three years he built his luxury castle. He claimed that he would protect the southern coast from pirates and the king's enemies—but no pirates ever came.

The visual impression is all-important at Bodiam. The approach to the castle requires the visitor to cross the bridge over the main river, pass the mill pond, and arrive at the moat and bridge (now destroyed) leading to the postern gate on the south. Convenient as the postern was, it was a servants' entrance, and no important person would use it. The visitors would continue around three sides of the moat, finally reaching a bridge leading to the main gate.

Figure 26. Bodiam Castle, England. Rising directly from the still water of a man-made lake, Bodiam is made more imposing by reflections that give the illusion of greater height to the walls. In this early photograph the abundant vegetation in the water reminds us of the use of the water defenses as part of the sanitary system of the castle. *Gramstorff Collection, Photographic Archives, National Gallery of Art, Washington, DC.*

Bodiam Castle has a symmetrical rectangular plan with crenellated cylindrical corner towers and a rectangular tower in the center of each side, one of which is a fortified gateway and one of which contains the postern gate. A slightly projecting chapel breaks the symmetry of the exterior. The principal domestic buildings lie directly across a square courtyard from the main gate. A passage leading to the postern also acts as a screens passage; as one enters, the hall is on the left and doors leading to the pantry, kitchen and buttery are on the right. The lord's residence is reached from the upper end of the hall, and beyond that are the guests' quarters and chapel. On the other side, beyond the kitchen, are quarters for servants. The military detachment was housed beside the entrance gate. The castle was beautiful, practical, and convenient. It includes thirty-three fireplaces and twenty-eight garderobes (which discharged directly into the moat, turning what is today a lily pond into an open sewer). Bodiam has been called "an old soldier's dream castle."

In Bodiam Castle's design we see a perfect example of symbolic architecture. Bodiam could never have withstood a siege. Luckily it was never tested. The castle was built in a low-lying place, where a small stream feeds the moat. An attacking enemy had only to cut through the earth embankment to drain the moat. Why then was the wide moat constructed? Aesthetic considerations must have played a role. The moat is like a small lake, and the building seems to rise directly out of the water, Reflected in the water, the castle seems to double in size.

Not only could the moat be drained quickly and easily, the walls were too low and too thin (between six and seven feet) to withstand bombardment. Furthermore, large windows in the hall and the chapel also destroyed any military effectiveness the walls might have had. The battlements on the walls and towers are purely decorative, for the crenels are not high enough to shield the men standing behind them. Finally, the higher ground around the castle made anyone on the wall-walks vulnerable to crossbow bolts.

These military features do serve a symbolic purpose. Sir Edward Dallyngrigge built his dream castle at a time when pageantry, excessive attention to the forms of chivalry, and tales of King Arthur and the Knights of the Round Table entertained and inspired the aristocracy. Sir Edward had no ancient tower, no ancestral castle like Kenilworth; he had to build his castle from the start, just as he built his own career and fortune. He was an important man in his own locality (he owned the market and a mill), but he was not a landed aristocrat. Just what his own fantasy or intention was in building Bodiam we do not know, but we can imagine that Sir Edward enjoyed the symbolism associated with military architecture. Bodiam's architectural forms are dictated not by function, but by an imaginary world. We have seen this contrast between reality and imagination in Rogier's painting *St. George and the Dragon* with which we began our excursion into the world of the Middle Ages (see Figure 1).

SYMBOLIC SETTINGS: WOODS, FORESTS, AND WATER MEADOWS

Royal and baronial castles continued to be built, but in the fourteenth century a new group of newly rich and politically powerful people began to take on the trappings of aristocratic behavior and to build castellated residences. While many castles dominate the countryside from hills and cliffs, these newer castles might also be built in woods, forests, or water meadows.

The forest castle served as a hunting lodge for noblemen and noble-women who engaged in the sport. At first the hunt with horses and hounds (a type of hunting known as the chase) kept hunters and their mounts in good physical condition for battle and incidentally augmented the food supply. Later, professional hunters provided most of the deer, boar, and rabbit meat for the cooks. Eventually hunting, as an exclusively noble sport, was surrounded by elaborate rituals. Even cutting up a deer and dividing the meat became a specialized skill, a ceremony known as "breaking the stag." Nobles fenced and walled large sections of woodland near their castles for their private use in hunts and severely punished peasants who poached game. The stories of Robin Hood and his band of outlaws in Sherwood Forest reflect the importance and exclusive use of the forests. (Later legends made Robin Hood a nobleman at the time of Richard the Lion Hearted.) Ladies could join in the hunt with falcons, that is, fowling, and the benefits of hunting with hounds versus birds could be the subject of lively discussion. As early as the eleventh century the image of a figure mounted on a horse and holding a falcon indicated noble status.

Meadows and wetlands may seem like strange places to build castles, but water was an effective barrier. Lake-bounded castles could be impregnable fortresses—unless the lake was artificial and someone cut the dam or dike. The lake castles put the walls beyond the reach of many war engines and prevented both direct assault and mining or sapping operations. Water-filled moats, ponds, and lakes not only protected castle walls, but also provided a natural sewage system, because garderobes could discharge directly into the water. Moats also provided a place to raise frogs and fish for food. Finally, we should not overlook the sheer beauty of the setting used so effectively at castles like Leeds (see Figure 24), Bodiam (see Figure 26), and Kenilworth (see Figure 27). Reflections doubled the size of the image of the castle. Water also lent enchantment; then as now it had an almost magical appeal. The castles of Leeds southeast of London and Vincennes in the outskirts of Paris are typical of the new architecture and illustrate the forest and water meadow sites.

Leeds Castle

Contemporary with Bodiam is Leeds Castle (see Figure 24). Built at the end of the thirteenth century on two islands on an artificial lake set in an extensive meadow and woodland, Leeds Castle, like Bodiam, seems to rise from the water. The building of a gloriette on the smaller of the islands recalls Moorish buildings in Spain, the home of Eleanor of Castile, queen of England when Leeds was being built. In Spain, water played a large part in palace and garden architecture. At Leeds the broad lake formed by a dam reflects the castle's lime-washed walls. The dam also created a mill race that powered a grain mill, which was fortified as part of the barbican.

The story of the contested ownership of Leeds Castle gives an idea of how much it was appreciated. Bartholomew de Badlesmere, one of Edward II's courtiers, in 1318 exchanged property worth three times as much for the pleasure and convenience of living at Leeds. But Edward II's French wife, Queen Isabella, wanted the castle herself. In 1321 when Badlesmere was away, Isabella arrived at Leeds with her retinue and demanded entry. Margaret Lady Badlesmere refused to admit the queen. So began a confrontation between two strong-minded women. To allow the queen to enter would jeopardize the ownership of the castle, so Lady Badlesmere barred the gate. The queen, following French precedent, expected all castles to be open to her, and considered a closed gate an insult. A fight broke out between the castle guard and the royal party in which some of the queen's men were killed. King Edward sent in troops, and Lady Badlesmere had to surrender her home. She was imprisoned in the Tower of London and only released in 1322 after her husband's death. Left with neither home nor income, Margaret de Badlesmere and her young son Giles petitioned the queen and council to give Leeds back. Isabella, now the queen mother and regent, kept Leeds but gave Margaret another more valuable but less prestigious property.

Vincennes

In the thirteenth century King Philip Augustus built a manor house in the royal forest of Vincennes near Paris. Charles V (1364–80) in turn rebuilt this hunting lodge as a castle with the great tower we see today, finishing it in 1370. Like many fourteenth-century castles, it had a rectangular plan with walls, moat, corner towers, and central gateways but was not designed to withstand a serious siege. A residential tower standing in the middle of the west wall and an independent defensive system of walls and moat make the chateau of Vincennes secure against treachery. A chapel resembling the Ste.-Chapelle in the royal palace in Paris stood in the courtyard. Begun in 1379, it was not finished until 1552.

The tower house at Vincennes is a masterpiece of fourteenth-century architecture. The tower with its battlements stands about 170 feet high. Each floor has a single large room with a central pier supporting a stone vault. Corner towers provide space for additional small rooms and garderobes. Spiral stairs provide access to the six floors and roof. A large ceremonial stair leads from the second floor entry to the royal residence and to a chapel on the third floor. Lords attending the king occupied the fourth floor, and the fifth floor provided lodging for servants. The top floor and roof line are battlemented and the space is entirely given over to military use.

SYMBOLIC CEREMONIES: PUBLIC AND PRIVATE

The late Middle Ages saw the increase in desire for private spaces, as well as domestic comfort. The great hall still formed the focal point of castle life and architectural design and the stage for ceremony and feasting (Documents 68 and 69). The lord and lady of the castle and their guests seated at the high table were served a banquet of three to five courses, each of which might have as many as fifteen dishes. Those at the tables in the hall usually had a buffet with much less food. Heavy food was served first and delicacies and sweets at the end. Wine was the usual drink; spiced wine was served at the end of the feast. Between the last courses spectacular displays of food, such as swans or peacocks that had been roasted and then returned to their skin and feathers, might be presented. At this time live human actors might perform skits or juggling or gymnastic acts. From the minstrel's gallery over the screens passage musicians entertained. The musicians might be in the permanent employ of the castle or they might wander from place to place, and so they also brought the latest news and gossip. In the fifteenth century they even organized into guilds.

The Closet

After festivities in the hall, people might retire to more intimate surroundings, moving through the building and arriving at ever more exclusive spaces and controlled entries. Personal safety had something to do with the design, to be sure, but also the dramatic ritual performance of everyday activities. Two special areas developed—the closet (the word for study) and the private garden ("secret" garden in Italy). The closet was the lord's private space; it was in fact a small room with space for only one or two confidants. The closet might also house a small library and a treasury of rare, precious, or wonderful objects. To retire to the lord's closet allowed the most confidential conversation.

The Pleasure Garden

The castle pleasure garden was an equally private place. The symbolism of the Garden of Eden, Song of Songs, and Paradise or royal hunting park permeates its design and plantings. With increased security—and for some people, increased leisure—the pleasure garden became a necessary adjunct to a palace. Stairs often led from the ladies' apartments directly into the garden. Private, walled, with turf-covered benches, arbors and special trees for shade, flowers to delight the eye and nose, and even a fountain to cool a wine jug and refresh the senses, the pleasure garden was a wonderful place. Here one could hold confidential conversations and indulge in amorous adventures. Expenses for exotic plants like lemon trees, for majolica tiles, and for rose bushes hint at the beauty and luxury of this most ephemeral art.

Tournaments

Theatrical performances, in which the guests might join, sometimes with tragic results, became very important by the fifteenth century. Then as now people loved to dance. They also loved sports, hunting, and especially tournaments (Document 63). Tournaments began as training for warfare. The space between castle walls known as the lists provided space for military exercises and also for jousting. Jousting was a formal fight, engaged in as a sport. In the twelfth century two teams of knights engaged in a free-for-all combat called a melee, a word we still use for a chaotic situation. Weapons were supposed to be blunt, but injuries and even deaths were common. In the thirteenth century tournaments provided entertainment that included spectacular athletic displays, colorful rituals, and banquets. William Marshall, lord of Pembroke Castle, began his career as a jouster in tournaments.

By the fourteenth century the jousts consisted of formal contests in which mounted warriors charged each other with lances in an attempt to knock each other off the horse. Heralds supervised the tournament and acted as umpires. Jousting took place in walled lists. Temporary wooden walls could be constructed to form the lists, or the area between the inner and outer walls of a castle could serve. Spectators watched from the castle walls, which might be extended with temporary wooden barriers, or "tilts." Pavilions and stands for spectators were also built.

In the fifteenth and sixteenth centuries tournaments became a very expensive sport, engaged in only by wealthy men who wore splendid armor identified by heraldic colors and emblems. They rode powerful horses (destriers) that were also decked out with heraldic trappings. Kings even held international competitions in which they guaranteed safe conduct for jousters from abroad. In 1344 at a tournament at Windsor Castle, men came from Scotland, France, Burgundy, and elsewhere. The knights fought for honor and glory, and they often dedicated their skill and strength to their ladies, who judged and awarded prizes. Ceremony and spectacle replaced mock warfare.

Heraldry

Heraldry began as a system of personal identification that enabled knights to identify friends and foes in battle (Document 66). Each man adopted a color and easily recognizable pattern or image to place on his shield; this became his coat of arms and made him recognizable when fully armed. Women also adopted coats of arms. We have noted the castle emblems of Queen Blanche of Castile. The complex patterns of heraldry required highly trained specialists who not only identified owners but also made sure that each design was unique. Heralds had an official organization and training program, and they kept records of coats of arms. Eventually, coats of arms decorated and identified armor, clothing, personal belongings, flags, banners, and buildings. Cities, states, guilds, associations, churches, and colleges adopted coats of arms. Gateways were decorated with shields and heraldic banners flew from towers.

FROM FORTRESS TO PALACE: THE CASTLE OF KENILWORTH

The Castle of Kenilworth carries to a logical conclusion the role of the castle as a symbol and setting for the dramas of life. Geoffrey de Clinton built the original castle in the twelfth century—probably a motte and bailey, with the motte where the stone tower stands today (see Figure 10). The town of Kenilworth and an abbey grew nearby. In the thirteenth century the king ordered the walls to be replaced with stone and an earthen dam to be made to form lakes and a marsh (the Great Mere) around the castle. The causeway leading to the castle gate also served as the tiltyard. The monastery used the water to fill its fish ponds. In the fifteenth century the marsh was transformed into a lake leading to a pleasance that could be approached by a boat. The pleasance could be a residence, a hunting lodge, or a pleasure palace.

In the thirteenth century, Simon de Montfort owned the castle. An active politician as well as a warrior, he helped set up the first parliament, led a failed rebellion, and died at the battle of Evesham in 1265. His followers escaped to Kenilworth, where the royal forces laid siege. Kenilworth, considered impregnable (like Richard's Chateau Gaillard), fell to the king's forces. The operation demonstrated yet again the weakness of the great tower in siege warfare. By the end of the century, as we have seen, commanders used castles as headquarters but fought in the open field.

In the late Middle Ages Kenilworth was transformed into a fabulous palace by its new owner, the younger son of King Edward II, John of Gaunt, Duke of Lancaster (1340–99). John of Gaunt had enormous power and wealth, which he chose to display in his architectural commissions. Through marriage to Constance, the daughter and heir of the Spanish king Peter the Cruel, John of Gaunt claimed the kingdom of Spain in 1369. He rebuilt Kenilworth as a true royal palace, with an extraordinary great hall, a private range of buildings on the south, and huge kitchens on the west side of the inner courtyard. Although severely damaged, the ruins allow us imagine the splendor of the original buildings.

Gaunt's enormous hall stands on the site of the earlier hall (Figures 27 and 28). The remaining stonework shows that it is an early example of the perpendicular style, where geometric tracery spreads over walls and windows to create the effect of paneling. All of John of Gaunt's build-

Figure 27. John of Gaunt's Hall, Kenilworth Castle, England. Across the wide courtyard from the great tower (see Figure 10) stands the great hall built in the 1380s. The addition of large windows to the great hall and the private chambers turned Kenilworth into a palace. *Photograph: Marilyn Stokstad.*

ings were built in this simple and efficient new style, giving a unity to the different building types. From the outside, two towers flank the hall and create a symmetrical composition although the spaces function differently. A long and impressive external stair from the courtyard up to the second floor entrance made a dramatic approach. These stairs lead up through a sculptured gatehouse into a waiting room and then into a huge hall. Inside the hall, tall windows open to both the courtyard on one side and the "great mere" on the other. From the seats flanking each window the visitor or guest could admire the lake and deer park but could not see the pleasance. Views and viewing platforms (there may have been such a platform at Kenilworth) were an important part of late medieval planning.

Staircases became important architectural features. A grand staircase was built in the royal palace in Paris, and can still be seen at the bishop's palace at St. David's, Wales (see Figure 25). After passing through an outer gate, one enters a vast open court and is confronted by not one but two enormous halls, each with a grand staircase. This magnificent palace suggests the imposing appearance of later medieval buildings.

In the sixteenth century, construction began again at Kenilworth. By

Figure 28. John of Gaunt's Hall, Kenilworth Castle, England, interior. The second-floor hall had huge windows looking out over a man-made lake. Deep embrasures would have created private spaces in the public hall. Because the floor is gone, one can see the change of masonry that marks the different levels. *Photograph: Marilyn Stokstad.*

the 1530s the monastery had been suppressed, and its stone was used to construct buildings in the town and castle. The timber from the buildings of the pleasance also was reused in the courtyard of the castle. New stables, visitor's quarters, and gatehouse were added; the Norman great tower was transformed with a gallery; and a formal Italianate garden was planted. Kenilworth became the site of the most spectacular pageantry of the Elizabethan age.

The Norman tower, although modernized with huge windows punched through its walls, played an important role in establishing the antiquity and importance of the family. The open gallery or loggia, on the other hand, demonstrated that they knew the latest fashions. The loggia, an amenity recently introduced from Italy, was known in England through pattern books. (The new technology of printing made the spread of ideas and images fast and easy.) From the loggia visitors could admire the formal gardens, just as they would in an Italian renaissance palazzo. Even the stair leading down into the garden was designed so that the garden could be admired at each landing and turning. The garden had fountains, topiary work (plants clipped into shapes), arbors, alleys of green grass, and carved obelisks, spheres, and sculptures of heraldic bears. A garden pavilion provided a comfortable place to sit and chat.

The finest moment in Kenilworth's history as a palace was the extraordinary party given by Robert Dudley, Earl of Leicester (1533–88), for Queen Elizabeth I. Elizabeth had given Kenilworth to him in 1563. Leicester organized an elaborate visit and entertainments for her in July 1575. When the queen arrived in the evening, she was welcomed by the "Lady of the Lake" who proclaimed that, in Elizabeth's honor, she arose from the lake for the first time since the days of King Arthur. The Lady of the Lake then recited the history of the castle. Along the causeway Leicester placed gifts for the queen.

Time stood still for the queen, or so said the earl, who stopped the hands of the giant blue and gilt clock on the Norman tower during the queen's visit. Gossips noted that Elizabeth did not emerge from her lodgings until five in the afternoon, but she was not resting. She worked so hard that twenty horses a day were needed to transport the paperwork between Kenilworth and London. Elizabeth was a conscientious ruler, although she played the role of the unattainable lady, the object of desire in the medieval game of courtly love. Architecturally, Kenilworth also alluded to past medieval glories. The palace-castle was the perfect stage setting for Elizabeth and her court.

Only fifty years after Leicester's festivities the royal drama came to an end. Oliver Cromwell's army blew up the great tower with gunpowder. Then his men destroyed and made the palace uninhabitable, and in 1649 the lakes were drained. But the romance of Kenilworth continued. Sir

Walter Scott's novel, *Kenilworth*, ensured its place in the public imagination, and today the place is a much-visited park-like ruin. With Kenilworth, the era of the castle as a fortress, home, or romantic setting comes to a close.

SUGGESTIONS FOR FURTHER READING

Coulson, Charles L. *Castles in Medieval Society, Fortresses in England, France and Ireland in the Central Middle Ages.* Oxford: Oxford University Press, 2003.

Creighton, O. H. *Castles and Landscapes.* London and New York: Continuum, 2002.

Emery, Anthony. *Greater Medieval Houses of England and Wales, 1300–1500.* Cambridge, UK: Cambridge University Press, 1996.

Johnson, Matthew. *Behind the Castle Gate; From Medieval to Renaissance.* London and New York: Routledge, 2002.

Pounds, N.J.G. *The Medieval Castle in England and Wales: A Social and Political History.* Cambridge, UK, and New York: Cambridge University Press, 1990.

Woolgar, C. M. *The Great Household in Late Medieval England.* New Haven: Yale University Press, 1999.

CHAPTER 5

IMPACT AND CONSEQUENCES: THE AFTERLIFE OF THE CASTLE

THE MILITARY AFTERLIFE OF THE CASTLE

At the end of the Middle Ages, castles began to lose their military function, but not their psychological impact as a symbol of authority. Gunpowder and cannons supported armies of mercenary troops, and the garrison forts built to house them adopted the crenellated walls of private aristocratic castles. By the sixteenth century, professional soldiers lived in barracks, a few officers and the governor had finer quarters, and kings and nobles merely directed the operations from distant palaces where battlements had become purely symbolic decoration. The Battle of Crecy between France and England in 1346 is traditionally considered to be the first use of cannons on the battlefield. At first the noise and smoke created by the explosion terrified horses and men, and wreaked more havoc than the projectiles. Early cannons could be more dangerous for the gunners than for the enemy, but military engineers rapidly developed the weapons' power and accuracy. A castle's high walls and towers made easy targets for gunners whose power and accuracy reduced once formidable medieval buildings to rubble. Mining became more successful because the attackers could put explosives under the walls.

Changing Castle Design

With cannons, siege warfare and castle design had to change. Stone-throwing machines were still very effective, but the prestige attached to cannons because of their novelty and their enormous expense made them the ultimate royal armament. These early cannons could be fired only ten or twenty times an hour and had to be cleaned after every shot and regularly cooled. They were effective only at about fifty yards. Cannons required massive earthworks to absorb the shock of firing.

Mons Meg, the six-ton cannon still to be seen in Edinburgh castle, was cast in 1449 in Flanders for the duke of Burgundy, who presented it to the Scottish king in 1457. Mons Meg could fire gunstones that weighed 330 pounds nearly two miles, but the cannon was so heavy it took 100 men to move it and then they could move it only at a speed of three miles a day. The Scottish kings used Mons Meg as a siege weapon for the next hundred years, as much for the impressive explosion it produced as for its actual usefulness. After about 1540 the cannon was only used to fire ceremonial salutes from Edinburgh castle walls. In 1681 the barrel burst and could not be repaired.

To counter the new offensive weapons, architects created a new system of defense in depth by using low, broad ramparts that were wide enough to endure firing from the enemy and at the same time support their own cannons and teams of gunners. Extremely thick masonry walls were expensive and slow to build, so wide and low earthen ramparts faced with stone became common. Since guns shoot horizontally, the land around the castle walls was cleared to form a space called the glacis. As we have seen at the castle of Angers, existing towers were cut down to the same height as the walls and turned into firing platforms (see Figure 17). This redesign of the towers did not "slight" the castle, but rather made it more effective in the new age of artillery warfare.

Batteries and Bastions

Between 1450 and 1530 Italian military engineers, architects, and theoreticians rethought castle design. To be most effective, guns were placed in batteries so that several cannons fired together at the same spot. Low, solid, D-shaped towers together with masses of masonry angled out from the walls served as supports for artillery and as observation platforms. This new form of military architecture was called the bastion system. At first the bastions had a pentagonal plan: two sides form a point facing toward the enemy, two sides slope back toward the wall, and the fifth side adjoins the wall. Protective ears protruded at the angles. A curtain wall joined two bastions so an enemy approaching the curtain wall came under fire from the flanking bastions, and each bastion protected its neighbor as well as the wall. The units could be repeated around a castle or city. The developed gun platforms were called a *bolwerk* in Dutch, and a *boulevard* in France. They were built as ramparts all around the castle or town often as a second line beyond the old walls. In the nineteenth century, when city walls and ramparts were removed and the space was turned into tree-lined avenues, the avenues continued to be called boulevards. Today one can trace the line of these defenses on a city map by following modern boulevards.

The Emerging Fortress

Based on geometry as much as local conditions, the design of bastioned fortresses became the province of specialists whose plans might be based on theory rather than topography. Italians devised wholly "rational" plans for fortresses and cities in which geometric figures, especially stars formed by lines of fire, determined the plan of glacis, wide moat, and ramparts. But the development of printing in Germany and soon throughout Europe meant that Italian theories and designs spread rapidly and relatively cheaply. The plans, beautiful as designs and drawings in themselves, were often too fanciful or expensive to be built.

The sixteenth century was an age of wide-ranging and talented theorists. Men we usually think of as painters and sculptors also designed fortifications. Leonardo da Vinci (1452–1519) worked in Milan from 1482 to 1498 for the ruling Sforza family on military and engineering projects. Leonardo also designed guns, crossbows, armored vehicles, submarines, a parachute, and a flying machine and made plans for fortresses. From 1502 to 1504 Leonardo worked in Florence as a military adviser, then returned to Milan to advise on castles from 1508 to 1513. From 1517 until his death in 1519 he lived in France in the service of Francois I. Another Italian, Francesco de Giorgio (1439–1502) wrote a treatise on military engineering with improved fortress designs, published in 1480. From 1480 to 1486 he served the Duke of Urbino, designing the fortifications of Urbino. By 1494 de Giorgio was working for the king of Naples and Sicily designing the fortifications in Naples. Even Michelangelo (1475–1564) was the military adviser to the city of Florence in 1529, and in 1547 he designed the Vatican defenses.

The leading architectural writers and theoreticians, like Leon Battista Alberti (1404–72), devised an ideal symmetrical plan for forts and cities. The Italians eventually settled on the five-point star as the ideal shape. The streets radiated out from a central command post or headquarters (or city center with market hall and church) with streets leading to gates or the bastions. Streets in concentric circles completed the internal division. The ideal plan did not allow for individual variations; consequently, it never developed successful cities, but it could be found in army installations. In the sixteenth and seventeenth centuries the Italian designs spread through Europe and the European colonies.

The French architect and military engineer Sebastien Le Prestre de Vauban, who built major fortresses on the French borders for Louis XIV, became the most skillful designer of fortresses using the bastion system. The first forts in the Americas—Louisburg in Nova Scotia, Canada, or Fort Augustine in Florida—are simple "provincial" examples of the Vauban fort. Fort McHenry in Baltimore, where *The Star Spangled Banner* was written, is a characteristic example of the bastion scheme with its central plan, wide earthen ramparts, bastions, and casemates. The Pentagon repeats the Renaissance five-sided, pentagonal plan with a central court, radiating street-like halls and concentric corridors. The castle design recommended by Leonardo da Vinci and Alberti has become the American headquarters and symbol of military power.

A FADING SYMBOL OF WEALTH AND AUTHORITY

The medieval castle had a long life as a symbol of wealth and authority, as a stage on which an increasingly irrelevant aristocracy could play out their rituals of power, and as a symbol of lineage and a reminder of a glorious past. Shakespeare in his history plays glorified the rise of the Tudor dynasty out of the struggles of the houses of York and Lancaster. In *Henry V*, soldiers Gower, Fluellen, Macmories, and Jermy at the siege of Harfleur argue whether mining and blowing up walls accords with "the discipline of war." Meanwhile Cervantes in 1605 put finish to the pretensions of chivalry with his delusional knight Don Quixote of la Mancha, tilting at windmills on the central Spanish plains.

THE CASTLE BECOMES A PALACE

In the sixteenth century, castles became palaces. Along the Loire river and its tributaries the French built graceful palaces ever more divorced from military reality, meanwhile in the south, Spain and Portugal—inspired in part by the luxury of Moorish palaces and the availability of skilled Moorish craftsmen—created architecture that gave rise to the dreamers' "castles in Spain." Vestiges of medieval battlements decorated the buildings, which were now built for comfort and display.

Chenonceau

Chenonceau, the archetypical Loire chateau, was begun in 1512 when Thomas Bohieu bought the old castle of Chenonceau and demolished the existing building except for the great tower. The tower still stands in front of the entrance to the chateau. Between 1513 and 1521, while Thomas was engaged in his work as a tax collector for King Charles VIII, Catherine Breconnet, his wife, oversaw the building project (Figure 29). The palace-castle stands on piers of a former mill on the river bank. The builders paid homage to the castle form by adding sham battlements, steep roofs, dormers, gables, and corner turrets with conical roofs to what is essentially a simple rectangular building. The library and chapel are corbelled out over the water, but they are the only elements breaking through the flat walls. Service areas, such as the kitchen and storage, are below water level in the supporting piers. The builders had little time to enjoy their home, and when they died their son gave the chateau to Francis I (1515–47) in payment for debts. The king used the property as a hunting lodge. The French king Henry II (1547–59) gave the chateau to his mistress, the famous beauty Diane de Poitiers. Diane was intelligent and practical as well as beautiful, and she turned the castle lands into a very profitable agricultural estate and planted formal pleasure gardens beside the moat and river.

The next resident, Catherine de Medici, devoted herself to a rich and worldly lifestyle, using Chenonceau as a place to hold magnificent parties. The bridge across the river with its two-story gallery was built later by Philibert Delorme for Catherine de Medici. Francis II (1559–60) and his bride Mary Stuart (Mary, Queen of Scots) as well as Charles IX enjoyed Catherine's hospitality. On one occasion, the moat became the setting for choirs of young women who, dressed as nymphs, splashed in its water and then danced through the gardens pursued by young men disguised as satyrs. Fireworks over the river officially ended the evening's entertainment.

Scottish Tower Houses

The turrets and battlements of a French chateau also seem to sprout from the tops of Scottish tower houses, recalling the old alliance between Scotland and France. Like the Norman towers, these tower houses had their principal rooms and entrance on the second or even third floor. One or two projecting wings might be built to add additional spaces giving the plan a distinctive Z shape. A low wall enclosed a courtyard, called a barmkyn, with ranges of lodgings for retainers. The owner lived in the tower, not just as a matter of prestige but also for safety. The top of the building could be quite elaborate with a large hall surrounded on the exterior with two levels of battlements, whose machicolations and turrets were corbelled out over the walls. So popular were tower houses in Scotland that they continued to be built into the seventeenth century, with splendid examples like Craigevar and Crathes.

In the far north not far from Aberdeen in Scotland, the merchant William Forbes built his tower house at Craigevar, finishing it in 1626 (Figure 30). The Scottish "lairds" (landholders, not necessarily noble "lords") topped their towers with turrets, gables, and miniature battlements inspired by their French allies. Not only did they pierce the tower walls with little round holes, just the right size for a gun barrel, they also carved their water spouts in the shape of tiny stone cannons. These Scottish tower houses inspired the "Scottish Baronial" style of the nineteenth century, epitomized by the royal holiday residence, Balmoral Castle.

Sir Walter Scott in Scotland, Alfred, Lord Tennyson and Angustus Pugin in England, and Viollet-le-Duc and Victor Hugo in France, not only re-created medieval architecture, they also inspired generations with their novels, poetry, and scholarly writing. They helped to save the castles and monasteries as evidence and reminders of their countries' past.

The Medieval Revival

A study of chivalry and its ideals led some people to see the Middle Ages as superior, morally, to their own times. They identified with the

Figure 29. Chateau, Chenonceau, France. Built on the River Cher, a tributary of the Loire, the Chateau of Chenonceau is a country pleasure palace that pays tribute to earlier castles by using details of military architecture in its decoration. The turreted building dates from the early sixteenth century, and the bridge extending to the left from midcentury, in full classical Renaissance style. *Photograph: Karen Leider.*

past, a past that they invented as an ethical ideal. The study of the medieval past, they believed, would provide examples—and inspiration—for their own times. They preserved crumbling walls as romantic ruins, and they built new medieval castles on the foundations of the past. To be sure, many eighteenth century intellectuals looked to a golden age of Greece and Rome, but in the nineteenth century with the growth of na-

Figure 30. Tower house, Craigevar, Scotland. Scotland and France were old allies, and the Scottish tower house often seems to have a French chateau grafted onto the top of a simple square tower. The military aspects of the building have become almost entirely decorative. *Photograph: Karen Leider.*

tionalism, people in England, France, Germany, and Scandinavia sought inspiration in their own national past. The gentleman of the nineteenth century identified with the ideals of the medieval knights, exemplified by the court of King Arthur, where all men were noble and brave and all ladies were chaste and beautiful (Document 1). In this imaginary middle ages, everyone had a place in society: the aristocrats were virtuous and chivalrous; the peasants were loyal and hard working; the clergy, pious; the judges, fair. They came together in the castle's courtyard and hall. Surely, the idealists thought, the ideals of chivalry controlled passions and enforced virtue, self-sacrifice, and self-control. They saw the Middle Ages as wholesome and natural, a patriarchal society in which every person had privileges and responsibilities. How far from reality was their dream of times gone by.

The romantic revival of medieval styles in architecture and decoration led to splendid and original forms in castles and castle decoration, and also to the appreciation and preservation of real castle architecture. The Tower of London's White Tower was surrounded by functional modern buildings. Windsor castle took on the magnificent form we see today designed for King George IV and Queen Victoria and Prince Albert. In the south, the Duke of Norfolk built a magnificent neo-Gothic home at Arundel, which nearly dwarfs the ancient mound and tower. Modern castle building reached its height in William Burgess' Cardiff Castle built for the third Marquis of Bute beside a fine twelfth-century tower. And in north Wales, Thomas Hopper, the architect for the immensely wealthy George Pennant's Penrhyn Castle, began work in 1827 and finished the "Norman" castle fourteen years later. Since Pennant's wealth came from slate, that material was used extensively in the castle.

The Eglinton Tournament

Medievalism as a cult was demonstrated rather dramatically by young aristocrats in the nineteenth century. The extraordinary lengths to which the medieval revival could go reached the height of glamour and folly in the Eglinton Tournament held August 29 and 30, 1839. Archibald Montgomery, the 13th Earl of Eglinton, inspired by his stepfather Sir Charles Lamb who was the Earl Marshall of England, decided to re-create a fourteenth-century tournament at his estate near the Scottish coast, southwest of Glasgow. He invited dozens of friends to take part, and thirteen of them actually agreed to participate as knights. Lord Eglinton acted as Lord of the Tournament; Sir Charles Lamb, as Knight Marshall; and the Marquis of Londonderry was King of the Tournament. Women also had roles to play, for example, as the Queen of Beauty and her ladies. Lord Eglinton hired a professional designer to build pavilions and stands and to advise participants on their costumes. The men spent all summer learning to joust and practicing their roles.

On the great day of the tournament, thousands of spectators mobbed the estate in spite of a drizzling rain. By the time the tournament should have begun with the grand parade to the lists, the rain turned into a downpour, soaking costumed participants and destroying their plumes and banners. One of the leading contenders, the Marquis of Londonderry, fearing for the state of his armor and splendid costume including an elaborate plumed headdress, rode onto the field protecting himself with a large umbrella. This ludicrous sight turned the elaborate pageant into a farce. The unfortunate Marquis became famous as "The Knight of the Umbrella." Needless to say the tournament came to an abrupt halt. The jousts were held the next day, and the affair concluded with a banquet at which time (to the surprise of no one) the Earl was proclaimed the winner. The ideals of chivalry appealed to the nineteenth-century aristocrats, and some notion of Gothic imagery became a part of popular culture, but no one tried to hold another open-air tournament.

The Romance of the Middle Ages

As we laugh at the idea of a knight carrying an umbrella, we should recall the popular Renaissance festivals of our own time as well as the jousting matches that entertain crowds in air-conditioned lists in places like Excalibur in Las Vegas. The members of the Society for Creative Anachronism attempt to re-create accurately the armor and weapons, the tournaments and festivals, but also the utilitarian arts and the food and dress of the past. Other people are constructing and testing stone-slinging machines, practicing archery with long bows, forging swords, and building new "medieval" castles. Castles inspire children's toys and adult fantasies. Theme parks have their late medieval architecture of crenellated towers and walls, turrets with witches' hat roofs, monster-filled moats crossed by drawbridges leading to gatehouses with portcullises opening into a fantasy land as extravagant as Lord Eglinton's tournament.

The dream castle remains part of the twenty-first-century fantasies of life in the twelfth and thirteenth centuries. The towers of the Alcazcar of Segovia took on a second life as the witch's castle in Walt Disney's film version of Snow White. Fantasy lands and theme parks build crenellated turrets. Castles have become a business. They lure and beckon tourists with reenactments around the walls, banquets in the ancient halls, and tea and souvenirs in the stables. And one need only drive through an American suburb to see towers, miniature crenellations, and conical witches' hat roofs rising above wooden houses set in manicured lawns. The castle has had a remarkable afterlife.

Who would have thought that the grim mass of a great tower or the chamber block of a complex twelfth-century castle would inspire the imagination of people so many centuries later? Who would guess that people living in heated and air-conditioned buildings with glass in the windows, carpets on the floors, refrigerators and microwave ovens in the kitchen, running hot water in the showers and laundries, and flushing toilets would look back with nostalgia to the hard life experienced by people in the Middle Ages? But the sheer magnificence of castle architecture, the almost overwhelming fascination of ruined towers, the labyrinthine patterns of earthworks and crumbling walls still capture our imagination.

SUGGESTIONS FOR FURTHER READING

Johnson, Matthew. *Behind the Castle Gate; From Medieval to Renaissance*. London and New York: Routledge, 2002.

Mancoff, Debra. *The Arthurian Revival in Victorian Art*. New York: Garland Publishing, 1990.

Simpson, W. Douglas. *Castles in England and Wales*. London: Batsford, 1969.

Toy, Sidney. *A History of Fortification from 3000 B.C. to A.D. 1700*. New York: Macmillan, 1955.

BIOGRAPHIES

AUTHORS

Anna Comnena (1083–died sometime after 1148),
Byzantine Princess
The Alexiad **(the history of the reign of Alexius I,**
1081–1118)

An intelligent and well-educated princess, Anna Comnena wrote an account of the Byzantine Empire and the reign of her father, Emperor Alexius I (1081–1118). Anna was born in 1083, the oldest of seven children. In 1097 she married Nicephorus Bryennius, a cultured historian and orator, not a military man. She said that she married only to please her parents, but the couple seems to have been congenial. Anna wrote about her husband in flattering terms and mourned his death in 1137. When Alexius died in 1118, and the Empress Irene in 1123, her brother John became emperor and ruled until 1143. Anna retired from active political and social life and devoted herself to writing the history of her times. She was still working on her book in 1148. Her date of death is unknown.

Anna was an excellent observer and judge of character. Her evaluations of political leaders and her comments on political and military events are astute and often witty. Her firsthand account of the western crusaders and their relations with the Byzantines make a fascinating contrast to the western chronicles. Anna neither liked nor trusted the western leaders, especially the Norman crusader Bohemund, whom she saw as merely a handsome barbarian. Her descriptions of sieges and the siege engines provide a remarkably detailed picture of this aspect of medieval warfare.

The Venerable Bede (c. 672/73–735), *Monk of Wearmouth and Jarrow*
Ecclesiastical History of England (from the Roman invasions to 731)

Bede was born in Northumbria, in northern England, in 672 or 673. At the age of seven he entered the monastery of St. Peter at Wearmouth, which was ruled by the learned and well-traveled abbot Benedict Biscop. In 685 Bede moved to the new twin monastery of St. Paul at Jarrow, where he spent the rest of his life. A deacon at seventeen, Bede became a priest at age thirty, and he is known to history as the Venerable Bede. He died in 735 and was buried at Jarrow; however, his remains were later moved to the cathedral in Durham. In writing his history of the Anglo-Saxons, Bede combined information gleaned from his monastery's extensive library, from letters and traditions, and from his own knowledge of current events and important people. He also wrote sermons, theology, biography, and poetry. He rarely mentions architecture.

The Anglo-Saxon Chronicle is an anonymous chronological list of events in England from the Roman invasions to 1154. It was based on authorities such as Bede and on royal and church records. The length and quality of the entries varies, but they usually include information on rulers, events, the weather and crops, and sometimes the condition of the people, such as the distress caused by castle building.

Jean Froissart (1337–after 1404), *Historian, Poet and Courtier*
Chronicles of England, France, Spain and the Adjoining Countries: From the Latter Part of the Reign of Edward II to the Coronation of Henry IV, 1327–c. 1400

Froissart was born in Valenciennes and educated in the Church, and entered the service of the counts of Hainaut (in modern Belgium). Although his family was not noble, he spent his life in the courts of Europe. In 1361 he moved to London as a secretary to Queen Philippa of

Hainaut, the wife of Edward III. Since he also served the Black Prince and the duke of Clarence (Chaucer's patron), he traveled to Scotland, southern France, northern Italy, and Rome. This experience gave him a view of Europe afforded few writers of the period. When he returned home after the queen's death in 1369, he soon found work with important patrons such as the count of Blois and the duke of Luxembourg and Brabant. Froissart became a priest and in 1384 a canon at Chimay and later at Lille. During the winter of 1388–89 he served at the court of Gaston Phoebus, count of Foix (d. 1391), a poet and man of letters.

Froissart wrote a history of Europe from the reign of Edward III to the death of Richard II. In that history, Froissart provides a detailed but somewhat idealized account of the first phase of the Hundred Years War. Although his history is filled with fascinating anecdotes, Froissart's point of view is decidedly on the side of his aristocratic patrons, whose lives he sees as glamorous and noble. He constantly checked and revised his history in an attempt to be accurate and at the same time please his patrons. Froissart also wrote poetry and romances. Nineteenth-century writers relied heavily on his narrative as they wrote their own romantic novels on medieval subjects.

Geoffrey of Monmouth (active 1129–55), *Administrator* *History of the Kings of Britain* (from Aeneas and the Trojans to the death of Cadwallader in 689)

In 1129 a man named Geoffrey signed as a witness for the foundation of a monastery at Osney. He must have been Welsh, because he calls himself "of Monmouth," but we do not know the place or date of his birth. Between about 1129 and 1150 he was an Augustinian canon of St. George's College in Oxford, where in 1138–39 he wrote his history. He did not become a priest until just before 1152, at which time he became bishop of St. Asaph's, the poorest and least important bishopric in Britain. Geoffrey died in 1155.

Geoffrey turned his talents to history and literature, and he dedicated his works to powerful men, probably in hopes of profiting from this common form of flattery. He dedicated his *History of the Kings of Britain* to Robert, Earl of Gloucester, the son of King Henry I. In his history he relied on sources such as Bede and William of Malmesbury as well as on legends, folk tales, and local traditions. He even claimed to have inside information on the history of Celtic Britain from an early British book, a book which has never been identified and may not have existed. Later historians considered Geoffrey to be merely a writer of fables, and today we turn to his history as a source for such stories as the tales of King Arthur and King Lear.

Giraldus Cambrensis (Gerald of Wales, c. 1146–1223), Churchman and Diplomat
The Topography of Ireland, 1187
The History of the Conquest of Ireland, 1187–89
The Itinerary through Wales, c. 1207
The Description of Wales, before c. 1203, expanded about 1207

Giraldus Cambrensis, a member of the distinguished Fitzgerald family, was born in the castle of Manorbeer near Pembroke, Wales, in 1146. His grandfather was the constable of Pembroke Castle. He lived and studied with his uncle, David Fitzgerald, bishop of St. David's, until at age twenty he went to the university of Paris. Giraldus returned home in 1180, and in 1184 King Henry II made him one of his chaplains and tutor to his son Prince John.

Giraldus served the king on diplomatic missions and accompanied Prince John to Ireland in 1185. His travels gave him the opportunity to collect information for his books on Ireland. Later Giraldus accompanied the archbishop of Canterbury on a journey through Wales, and again he wrote about his experiences and observations. He was with Henry II when the king died at Chinon in France, and the new king, Richard the Lion Hearted, at once employed him as a diplomat and administrator. Three times the chapter of St. David's elected Giraldus bishop (the most important Church position in Wales), but each time the king turned down the appointment. When King John finally offered him the post in 1215, he refused and retired from public life. He died in 1223.

Although observant and curious about people, places, and events, Geraldus was too credulous, and perhaps too loyal to Wales, to be a good historian. He recorded the tall tales, stories, legends, and popular lore that he heard on his travels, making his books fascinating to read but unreliable as evidence. Unlike most medieval writers, who wrote only about the aristocracy, Giraldus recorded everyday activities—Welsh hospitality, love of singing and harp music, jokes and tricks—and he described simple wooden houses and flower gardens as well as castles.

Jean, Lord of Joinville (1225–1317), *Grand Marshall (seneschal) of Champagne*
Chronicle of the Crusade of St. Louis, begun in 1272, second part 1298–1309, completed in October 1309

Joinville was born in 1225, lord of the castle of Joinville. He joined King Louis IX on the Fourth Crusade in 1248 and returned to France in July 1254. He wrote his memoirs late in life and only finished his work in 1309. Consequently, although his history is a firsthand account, he was writing from the perspective of an eighty-five-year-old, reminiscing about his glorious, and sometimes not so wonderful, past. He fills his memoirs with details, anecdotes, and descriptions of people and places, and so he gives us a vivid picture of the Holy Land and the crusaders' life. He idealized his leader, Louis IX, and was clearly proud to be his friend and companion in arms. He also wrote sympathetically about Louis' heroic wife, Margaret of Provence, and his domineering mother, the dowager queen Blanche of Castile.

Lambert of Ardre, *Priest and Local Historian, Writing between 1206 and 1229*
The Chronicle of Guines and of Ardre, from c. 918 to c. 1203

Lambert spent his rather uneventful life in the region of Guines, as the devoted priest of the local lords of Guines and Ardre. He was married and had two sons who worked with him and a daughter who married the illegitimate son of the lord of Ardre. He wrote his history of the family at the request of Arnold of Ardre, the son of his lord Baldwin II. Arnold had been excommunicated for destroying a mill belonging to a widow. Now Arnold wanted to marry a wealthy heiress, Beatrice of Bourbourg, but first he had to be reinstated into the Christian community. Lambert inadvertently insulted Baldwin by refusing to ring the church bells to announce Arnold's absolution before receiving an official notification, an action that would have been contrary to Church regulations. The family history may have been an attempt to return to the good graces of his lord. We are the richer for Arnold and Lambert's troubles because the *Chronicle* is a fascinating account of life in the eleventh and twelfth centuries.

Naturally, Lambert flattered his patron and dedicated the book to Arnold; nevertheless, Lambert seems to have tried to write an accurate account of his region. He had access to church records and consulted other people for their memories of local traditions and legends. Lambert had an essentially secular point of view, and attributes events to human action, not miracles. The lords of Guines were minor nobles living in the dune-land near Calais, but every detail of their family history was important to Lambert, who recorded such details as the bread tax instituted for the upkeep of a popular town bear. In his detailed descriptions of buildings and towns he notes the use to which buildings and even rooms in buildings were put, and so provides historians with valuable information.

Ordericus Vitalis (1075–c.1142), Monk of St. Evroult
The Ecclesiastical History of England and Normandy
(from the birth of Christ to the reign of Henry I of
England)

Ordericus Vitalis was born on February 15, 1075, in Attingham near Shrewsbury, England. His father was a follower and council member of Robert de Montgomery, the Earl of Shrewsbury. Ordericus tells us that he began his studies in Shrewsbury at age five, and when he was ten years old, his father sent him to Normandy, where he entered the scholarly Benedictine monastery of St. Evroult. Ordericus was soon recognized for his intelligence and love of learning. In 1086 he became a monk, taking the name Vitalis. He became a deacon and, in 1107, a priest.

Ordericus Vitalis spent most of his time in his monastery, studying and writing a history of Normandy and England. He traveled once to Worcester in England and once to Cambray in Flanders to collect historical evidence, and he also attended a general meeting of the Benedictine Order. He finished writing his history at the age of sixty-seven, and he probably died soon thereafter, perhaps in 1142.

As one would expect from a twelfth-century historian, Ordericus Vitalis began his history with the birth of Christ, but he rapidly moved from the history of Christianity to the history of his own times and place—England and Normandy. He called his work an ecclesiastical history, but we read his books for their insights into his own times. Ordericus included all the good stories he heard, as well as traditional lore, adventures, bits of scandal, and his own opinions, and he blended them all into a gripping tale. If you want to read the work of only one medieval historian, then Ordericus Vitalis is the author to choose. (See Chibnall, Marjorie. *The World of Orderic Vitalis*. Oxford: Clarendon, 1984.)

BUILDERS

Blanche of Castile (1188–1252), *Queen of France, 1223–26; Regent For Her Son during His Minority and While He Was on Crusade*

Blanche, the daughter of Eleanor of England and Alfonso VIII of Castile, and granddaughter of Eleanor of Aquitaine and Henry II, married prince Louis of France when she was twelve. Queen at last in 1223, her reign was short, for Louis VIII (1223–26), although an excellent warrior, died on the Albigensian crusade. Blanche became regent for her son Louis IX, over the objections to her as a woman and a foreigner. She asserted her authority over the barons, and by pursuing a policy of never aligning herself with a single faction, she kept the barons divided against each other and retained control in her own hands. She even kept France out of disastrous wars with England and Germany. Even when Louis came of age Blanche continued to be his closest adviser. Nevertheless, she did not always see eye to eye with Louis, and she disliked his wife, Margaret of Provence, whom he married in 1234. Devoted to her son Louis and his brothers Alphonse of Poitiers (1220–71) and Charles of Anjou (1226–85), she played politics to keep all of them in power in their respective territories. She rebuilt the castle at Angers into a magnificent seat of power. When Louis decided to go on a crusade, Blanche opposed his decision. Nevertheless, after four year of preparation, Louis left in 1248, and Blanche assumed the regency again. She died in 1252 while Louis was still in the Holy Land.

Blanche's patronage focused on the Cistercians and their strong yet severe art. The castle at Angers and other buildings usually attributed to the reign of Louis IX were often built during the regency and under the patronage of the regent-queen mother, Blanche.

Edward I (1239–1307), *King of England, 1272–1307;* *Duke of Aquitaine, 1272–1307*

Edward was first and foremost a warrior king. He was nearly killed while on crusade in Acre and learned he had inherited the throne while returning in 1272. He probably met his architect James of St. George as he passed through Savoy. Edward had married Eleanor of Castile, and the couple were crowned in 1274. For the next twenty years he stabilized the government at home and carried on a war against the Welsh, especially in 1277 and 1282–83 and finally in 1294–95. To control and govern Wales, Edward built a series of castles, of which the finest are Harlech, Conway, and Caernarfon. Edward made Caernarfon his principal headquarters.

In the 1290s his closest adviser and queen, Eleanor, died. At the same time trouble increased with France. In 1294 Philip IV tricked Edward into giving up Gascony by promising that the arrangement was temporary and that he, Philip, would return the land as the dowry of his sister Margaret. Of course Philip broke his promise at once. Edward married Margaret anyway in 1299, but Edward and Margaret did not get Gascony back until 1303.

Wars with Scotland cast a dark shadow over the last years of Edward's life. Edward defeated the Scots in 1296 and took the "Stone of Destiny" from Scone to London, where it was placed in the royal throne (and only returned in our own times). William Wallace led a successful rising in 1297, but the next year the English defeated the Scots and executed Wallace. Robert the Bruce, crowned king of Scots in 1306, led another revolt. On the way to fight the Bruce, Edward died in 1307.

Edward was a great patron of architecture, devoting thousands of workers and vast resources to building castles and fortification, additional work at Westminster Abbey and the royal palace, and a series of monuments to Eleanor, as well as stained glass and illuminated manuscripts.

Eleanor of Aquitaine (1122–1204), *Queen of France, 1137–52; Queen of England, 1154–89*

Eleanor inherited some of the richest land in France, the southwestern duchy of Aquitaine, in 1137. Her guardian, the French king Louis VI, immediately married her to his son and heir, the future Louis VII. Eleanor and Louis were distantly related, although the Church ignored the problem as long as possible. That Eleanor and Louis had little in common and did not care for each other would not have mattered in this period when marriages were arranged for political and financial advantage, but Eleanor had only daughters and the king had to have a male heir. In 1152 their marriage was annulled, and Eleanor departed rapidly for her own territory. In short order she married the young count of Anjou and duke of Normandy, Henry Plantagenet, and within a year gave birth to a son. In 1154 Eleanor and Henry became queen and king of England (1154–89). Two of the couple's sons survived their father to rule England—Richard the Lion Hearted (1189–99) and John (1199–1216).

Although not a castle builder, Eleanor was a patron of the arts. As queen of France she made gifts to the Abbey of St. Denis, including a precious crystal vase, and in England she brought an increased influence from Aquitaine on the visual arts as well as music and poetry. When she died in 1204, she was buried at the abbey of Fontevrault with her husband Henry II and her son Richard the Lion Hearted.

Henry I (1068–1135), *King of England, 1100–35*

Henry I became king of England in 1100 and duke of Normandy in 1106. As the third son of William the Conqueror, Henry had been passed over in the line of succession. When their father died in 1087, Robert inherited Normandy and William Rufus (r. 1087–1100), England. Robert pawned Normandy to William in order to raise money to go on the crusade. Before Robert could return, however, William died in a hunting accident, and Henry claimed the throne of England. Since Robert had not repaid his debt, Henry claimed Normandy, too. The brothers went to war, and Henry defeated Robert in 1106 and held him captive until his death in 1134. Henry had to contend with hostility and revolt the rest of his life. Henry's only legitimate son drowned in 1121, and Robert's son was killed in 1128. With no males to inherit, Henry turned to his daughter Matilda, who was married to the German emperor Henry V. The selection of Matilda instead of her cousin Stephen led to civil war and a period of anarchy in England that finally ended at midcentury with the accession of Henry II. Matilda later married Geoffrey Plantagenet, count of Anjou. Geoffrey was the son of Fulk, king of Jerusalem and builder of huge crusader castles. Their son was the formidable Henry II Plantagenet.

The period saw the construction of stone castles throughout the kingdom. The timber stockades and towers did not withstand the frequent wars of this period and were replaced by stone towers wherever the earth could support the weight.

Henry II Plantagenet (1133–89), *King of England, 1154–89*

In 1150 Geoffrey Plantagenet granted Normandy to his seventeen-year-old son Henry; when Geoffrey died in 1151, Henry also inherited Anjou. The next year Henry married Eleanor of Aquitaine, former wife of the French king Louis VII, a marriage that united western France above and below the Loire River. In 1154, Eleanor and Henry became rulers of England. Within five years Henry was at war with France, and from then on he was involved in conflicts everywhere. His struggle with Thomas à Becket began in 1160, and the archbishop's challenge to Henry's authority culminated in Becket's murder in 1170. In Thomas, England had a martyr and, in 1173, a saint. Then Eleanor and their sons, together with French nobles, rebelled in 1173 and again in 1188. In the east, from 1174 on, the Muslims under the leadership of Saladin reasserted their power, and the Christians suffered major defeats in 1187. Crusaders again rallied to march on Jerusalem.

Such troubled times saw the building and rebuilding of many castles, including Windsor Castle. During Henry II's reign a new style in art and architecture emerged in the churches around Paris and in southern England. Later it became known as the Gothic style, but at the time it was called "modern art" or "French work." Technically superior masonry vaults and effective new methods of buttressing vaults and walls permitted greater flexibility in design of buildings. Master masons and master carpenters were quick to capitalize on the new techniques. Castle and palace halls and chambers, as well as churches and other buildings, could be larger, with lighter walls and larger windows.

James of St. George (c. 1235–1308)

James of St. George, the designer and builder of Edward I's castles in Wales, learned the art of castle design from his father, who worked for the counts of Savoy. The counts were relatives of Edward I, and Count Amadeus served in the king's wars in Wales in 1277 and 1282. King Edward, in turn, had stayed at the count's castle of St. George, near Lyon, when he was returning home from the crusade in 1272. Master James of Savoy had built that castle and took the designation, "St. George," from it. Edward could have met or heard about Master James at that time. In 1282 James was working for Edward in Wales. Of the ten Edwardian castles he certainly worked on two and designed four more, including Caernarfon, Harlech, and Beaumaris. No two are alike and each is brilliantly adapted to the land and the local requirements. Master James perfected both the double enclosure wall design and the gatehouse as a residential fortress. As general designer and supervisor he had between 1,000 and 3,000 men working for him. They were brought in from all over England. Master James' stature among the masons is indicated by his high salary—he earned in a day what others earned in a week. When he finished Harlech in July 1290, Master James was awarded the honorary constableship of the castle. He retired with a pension and died in 1308.

John of Gaunt (1340–99), *Duke of Lancaster,* *1362–99; Claimed the Kingdom of Castile, 1372–88*

John of Gaunt (he was born in Ghent) was the son of Edward III, brother of Edward the Black Prince, and uncle of Richard II. John's marriage in 1359 to Blanche, daughter and heiress of the duke of Lancaster, made him duke of Lancaster in 1362. John spent his early years fighting in the French wars. He became one of the wealthiest and most powerful international figures of his time, a status reflected in his building projects. He owned twenty-nine castles, seven houses, and several hunting lodges, but his preferred residence was Kenilworth, which he built into a palace fortress worthy of his claims to royalty. After Blanche's death in 1368 John married Constance, the daughter of Peter the Cruel, king of

Castile. Peter had died in 1369, so in 1372 John of Gaunt claimed his wife's kingdom and prepared to wage war in Spain. He only gave up his claim to the throne in 1388 in exchange for a large annual payment from the Spanish king. Between 1373 and 1393 John and Constance spent significant sums to rebuild Kenilworth into a magnificent royal palace. Their building gave added impetus to the spread of the late medieval perpendicular style in architecture. Constance died in 1394 and John five years later (1399). John of Gaunt failed to become king of Spain, but his son Henry deposed Richard II and ruled England as Henry IV.

Louis VII (1120–80), *King of France, 1137–80*

In 1137 Louis married Eleanor of Aquitaine, and shortly thereafter Louis and Eleanor became king and queen of France. Eleanor's huge territory of southwest France joined the royal territories to create a powerful kingdom. Abbot Suger of St. Denis (1081–1151), the friend and trusted adviser of both Louis VI and Louis VII, guided the fortunes of the monarchy. When Louis and Eleanor left France to lead the Second Crusade, Abbot Suger acted as regent. Eleanor enjoyed the excitement of travel and the new experiences in the Holy Land, and by the time the king and queen returned home they both wanted their freedom. Louis needed a son to inherit the crown, and he blamed Eleanor for having daughters. As long as Abbot Suger lived, he was able to keep the couple—and their lands—together, but in 1152 the marriage was annulled, and Eleanor regained the lands she had inherited. Possibly Louis and his advisers did not expect that Eleanor would soon marry the count of Anjou, duke of Normandy, and heir to the English throne, Henry Plantagenet. In 1154 Henry and Eleanor became king and queen of England.

Louis married two more times—first Constance of Castile, who died in childbirth, and then Adele of Champagne. In 1165 Adele had a son and Louis at last had the required male heir, Philip Augustus.

Louis and his advisers changed the nature of the French monarchy from a feudal to a national government and the king became more of a public figure. The style and structural techniques of architecture changed just as dramatically. Again Abbot Suger was responsible. He gathered masons from different regions to build the abbey church, and in so doing he and his master masons created the new Gothic style.

Louis and Eleanor attended the dedication of Suger's abbey church in 1144.

Louis IX (St. Louis, 1214–70), *King of France, 1226–70*

Louis IX inherited the crown of France as a child in 1226. His mother, Blanche of Castile, took control of the government as regent until he came of age. She continued to advise him throughout his life, and she served as regent when he left on crusade in 1248. Politically Louis profited from the strong rule of Philip Augustus and the skillful politics of Blanche, but he had a constant struggle in southern France where nobles in league with England challenged his authority.

In 1234 Louis married Margaret of Provence, who attempted without success to replace his mother as his chief adviser. The two women disliked each other intensely. When ten years later Louis decided to go on crusade, Margaret accompanied him, leaving Blanche at home to govern France. After four years of preparation the king left in 1248 from his new southern bastide and port of Aigues Mortes. The crusaders arrived in Egypt, and after initial success in 1250 Louis was defeated, captured, and eventually ransomed. Although his brothers Alphonse and Charles returned to France, Louis stayed in the Christian Holy Land where he helped rebuild castles and towns. The news of his mother's death left him in despair, and in 1254 Louis returned to France, intending to rule as an ideal Christian king. He again decided to go on crusade, departed France in 1270, and arrived at Tunis, where he died. His bones were returned to France for burial at St. Denis. In 1297 the Pope declared him to be a saint.

During Louis' reign the Gothic style reached its finest expression. Architects created taller, lighter, more colorful buildings. They turned masonry structures into scaffolds formed of piers and buttresses supporting ribbed vaults that seemed to float overhead. Stained glass windows replaced walls. Residential buildings in castles became more comfortable and convenient as military and defensive aspects began to decline. Louis built a chapel in his palace to house the Crown of Thorns, which in 1239 he purchased from Baldwin II, the French ruler of Byzantium. The royal palace and the exquisite Ste.-Chapelle (1235–48) set the standard for royal residences for the rest of the century.

Philip II Augustus (1165–1223), *King of France,* *1180–1223*

Philip Augustus inherited the throne of France when he was only fifteen. A brilliant strategist, he outmaneuvered his Plantagenet rivals, and after the death of Richard the Lion Hearted in 1199 and the siege and surrender of Chateau Gaillard in 1204, Philip Augustus added Normandy to the royal territory. By the time he died in 1223, Philip Augustus had brought the lands north of the Loire River into the realm of France. He also gained control of the south after condoning a crusade against the Albigensians—the rich and cultured people of the south—under the guise of a crusade to stamp out heresy. The crusaders in many cases simply looted the country.

Philip Augustus was a bureaucrat and politician, not a warrior. He created a modern state in France, with a centralized government administered by members of the lesser nobility and bourgeoisie whose primary loyalty was to himself as king. By the time Philip Augustus died, he had put France on the road to becoming a unified nation rather than a collection of private territories, and he made Paris a true capital city. Philip Augustus saw the cities and the merchants and artisans as a new royal powerbase. He founded cities whose royal charters gave them special privileges; in return they provided the royal government with additional revenue. In Paris he built new city walls and royal palaces.

Philip IV the Fair (1268–1314), *King of France,* *1285–1314*

Philip IV, the grandson of St. Louis and called the handsomest man in Europe, surrounded himself with brilliant advisers and succeeded in reforming the government at home and expanding French power through Europe. Philip saw his grandfather as a model for Christian rulers; however, his own actions in expelling the Jews and the Italian bankers and suppressing the crusading order of Knights Templar (the royal bankers), as well as his controversies with the papacy, all seem motivated by money as much as by morality and belief. Philip's close relationship to Pope Clement V (1305–14) led to the establishment of the papal court in Avignon.

Philip continued the conflict with England, whose kings were legally his subordinates as the dukes of Aquitaine. He tricked Edward I out of the English holdings in the southwest, causing the two countries to engage in yet another war. As a condition of peace, Edward I married Philip's sister Margaret (1299), and Edward II (1307–27), his daughter Isabella (who so coveted Leeds Castle). These marriages proved to be unwise in the long run, for they permitted Edward III (1327–77) to claim France, and even Henry V's advisers could argue that Henry had a right to France through his great, great-grandmother Isabella.

Richard I the Lion Hearted (1157–99), *King of England, 1189–99*

Richard was born in 1157, the second son of Henry II and Eleanor of Aquitaine (his elder brother Henry died in 1183). Always energetic, he joined his mother in rebelling against Henry in 1173–74. As duke of Aquitaine, Richard established his authority in Aquitaine and then, in an alliance with Philip Augustus, he successfully claimed all of Henry's French territory. When Henry died in 1189, Richard became king of England, but he spent little time there. In 1190 Richard and Philip Augustus left on the Third Crusade. A brilliant commander and warrior, Richard the Lion Hearted defeated the Muslims, but he was frustrated in his attempt to recapture Jerusalem. In 1192 Richard made a treaty with Saladin that gave Christians access to Jerusalem and the holy sites. On his way home, Richard was captured and held for ransom by Leopold IV of Austria. Meanwhile Philip conspired with Richard's brother John to acquire Angevin lands. Richard was ransomed in 1193–94 and spent the rest of his life fighting Philip. Richard was a true son of Aquitaine, a troubadour in his own right. Two of his lyrics survive. He was wounded fighting while fighting wars in France at Chalus and died at Chinon. He was buried with his parents, Eleanor of Aquitaine and Henry II, at the abbey of Fontevrault.

With the pressure of constant warfare and under the influence of sophisticated Byzantine and Muslim design, European builders erected huge and effective castles and fortified cities and manor houses. Richard's castle Chateau Gaillard, a brilliant piece of military engineering built in 1196–98, was a key to Richard's confrontation with Philip. The castle was the last important design to use a true great tower. After Richard's death, Philip Augustus took the castle in 1204, but the English king, Henry V, regained the castle after a six-month siege in 1418.

William I the Conqueror (1028–87), *Duke of Normandy, 1035–87; King of England, 1066–87*

Born in 1028, in 1035 William inherited Normandy from his father Robert the Magnificent. Known as William the Bastard, he had to assert his authority over rival barons while still a youth. In 1050/51 William married Matilda of Flanders, the richest heiress in Europe, who was related to both the German emperors and the French king. William and Matilda formed a powerful political and family alliance. They had three sons and four daughters before 1066 when William left for England. While William was in England, Matilda ruled Normandy. William had to put down rebellions at home led by their son, Robert Curthose, in 1079 and 1083. When William died in 1087, he added to the political instability by leaving Normandy to Robert and England to William II Rufus. William Rufus died unexpectedly in 1100; a third brother, Henry, succeeded him and reestablished his father's combined territories.

After the battle of 1066, William spent the rest of his life on the move, securing the English territory by granting land to his Norman followers and building castles, something the Anglo-Saxons did not have. By 1100 historians and archeologists estimate that the Normans had built 5,000 castles and strongholds in England. To construct so many new fortifications in such a short time, the Normans used readily available and easily worked earth and timber and the motte and bailey design with a great timber tower. The Norman mottes, which are still visible as grassy mounds throughout England, effectively expressed the power and authority of the Norman rulers.

PRIMARY
DOCUMENTS

Primary documents provide firsthand accounts of castle life: how castles were built and how they were used, including the horrors of siege warfare. They also give us an insight into the lives of the people who lived in the castles and the nearby villages. Some of the authors write witty accounts filled with anecdotes and human interest; others report the facts as they knew them, although they occasionally add a poignant or perceptive detail. All of the writers capture the spirit of their times.

Many stories, which we come upon almost accidentally as we read, hint at complex tales. We long to know more. We are shocked at the cowardice displayed by the soldiers left to defend the castle of a hapless countess—men who deserted so rapidly that the invaders found the table set and food cooking in the kitchen (Document 23). We wonder about the education of the athletic Juliana, who not only shot a crossbow bolt at her father (she missed!) but also escaped her prison by swimming through the icy waters of the moat in winter, shockingly showing her naked legs (Document 52). We meet the two chatty countesses whose social call on the wife of the knight in charge of Lincoln castle provided cover for their husbands' sneak attack (Document 53). And we laugh at the fat, illiterate Bishop of Durham and his friends who were clever enough to sneak a rope into prison in a wine jug (just how large was that jug?) but forgot to make sure that the rope was long enough to reach the ground (Document 41). We sympathize with the bakers whose oven stood outside the castle walls and who had to go about their work of providing food while soldiers from both sides fought over the bread (Document 9). Our hearts go out to the crusader whose heart is so heavy that he cannot look back at his castle home as he leaves to join his king's war

(Document 11). And we recall our own homecomings as we sense the delight Gerald takes in writing about his visit to his home in Wales (Document 5). We like the duke's girl friend who warns him of treachery while shampooing his hair; he leaves so fast she doesn't have time to comb it out, but he saves her, too (Document 42). The tragic story of the dancers whose costumes catch on fire (Document 70) reminds us of the fires at crowded concerts in our own day, and the report of the spectators at sporting events cheering on their favorites (Document 63) also makes the distant past seem real.

Abbreviated references at the end of each document give the author's name and work. Students have expressed a strong preference for older translations over easier-to-read modern texts. They felt that the old-fashioned language gave a "medieval flavor" and was fun to read. Information about the writers has been included in Biographies; their works are listed in the Bibliography.

IN THE BEGINNING

DOCUMENT 1
King Arthur's Parents

And when the Easter festival drew nigh, the king bade the barons of the realm assemble in that city that he might celebrate so high a holiday with honour by assuming the crown thereon. All obeyed accordingly, and repairing thither from several cities, assembled together on the eve of the festival. The King, accordingly, celebrated the ceremony as he proposed, and made merry along with his barons, all of whom did make great cheer for that the King had received them in a joyful wise. For all the nobles that were there had come with their wives and daughters as was meet on so glad a festival. Among the rest, Gorlois, Duke of Cornwall, was there, with his wife Igerne, that in beauty did surpass all the other dames of the whole of Britain. And when the King espied her amidst the others, he did suddenly wax so fain of her love that, paying no heed unto none of the others, he turned all his attention only upon her. Only unto her did he send dainty tid-bits from his own dish; only unto her did he send the golden cups with messages through his familiars. Many a time did he smile upon her and spake merrily unto her withal. But when her husband did perceive all this, straightaway he waxed wroth and retired from the court without leave taken. . . .

. . . [T]he King gathered a mighty army together and went his way into the province of Cornwall and set fire to the cities and castles therein. But Gorlois, not daring to meet him in the field for that he had not so many armed men, chose rather to garrison his own strong places until such time as he obtained the succour he had besought from Ireland. And, for that he was more troubled upon his wife's account than upon his own, he placed her in the Castle of Tintagel, on the seacoast, as holding it to be the safer refuge. Howbeit, he himself betook him into the Castle of Dimiloc, being afeared that in case disaster should befall him both might be caught in one trap. And when message of this was brought to the King, he laid siege to Gorlois's castle.

The King besieged Tintagel castle. He wanted Igerne for himself and consulted his friend Ulfin who recommended that he ask Merlin to help him. Tintagel is described,

[T]here is no force that may prevail whereby to come unto her in the Castle of Tintagel? For it is situate on the sea, and is on every side encompassed thereby, nor none other entrance is there save such as a narrow rock doth furnish, the which three armed knights could hold against thee, albeit thou wert standing there with the whole realm of Britain beside thee. But, if Merlin the prophet would take the matter in hand, I do verily believe that by his counsel thou mightest compass they heart's desire.

Merlin uses his magical powers to disguise the king as Igerne's husband Gorlois

At last, committing the siege into charge of his familiars, he did entrust himself into the arts and mendicants of Merlin, and was transformed into the semblance of Gorlois. Ulfin was changed into Jordan, and Merlin into Brecil in such sort as that none could have told the one from the other. They then went their way toward Tintagel, and at dusk hour arrived at the castle. The porter, seeing that the Duke had arrived, swiftly unmade the doors, and the three were admitted. For what other than Gorlois could it be, seeing that all things seemed as if Gorlois himself were there? So the King lay that night with Igerne, for as he had beguiled her by the false likeness he had taken upon him, so he beguiled her also by the feigned discourses wherewith he did full artfully entertain her. For he had told her that he had issued forth of the besieged city for naught save to see to the safety of her dear self and the castle wherein she lay, in such sort that she believed him every word, and had no thought to deny him in aught he might desire. And upon that same night was the most renowned Arthur conceived, that was not only famous in later years, but was well worthy of all the fame he did achieve by his surpassing prowess.

Source: Geoffrey of Monmouth. *History of the Kings of Britain by Geoffrey of Monmouth*. Translated by Sebastian Evans. London: J. M. Dent; New York: E. P. Dutton, 1911. Ch. XIX, pp. 147–49.

DOCUMENT 2
The Roman Rampart, Built of Earth and Timber

[A]fter many great and dangerous battles, he [the Roman Emperor Severus, second century] thought it fit to divide that part of the island, which he had recovered from other unconquered nations, not with a wall, as some imagine, but with a rampart. For a wall is made of stones, but a rampart, with which camps are fortified to repel the assaults of enemies, is made of sods, cut out of the earth, and raised above the ground all round like a wall, having in front of it the ditch whence the sods were taken, and strong stakes of wood fixed upon its top. Thus Severus drew a great ditch and strong rampart, fortified with several towers, from sea to sea.

Source: Bede. *Bede's Ecclesiastical History of England. Also the Anglo-Saxon Chronicle*. Translated by J. A. Giles. London: George Bell, 1903. Bk. I, Ch. 4, pp. 10–11.

DOCUMENT 3
The Mound and Ditch Castles in Ireland Continue the Earth and Timber Building Traditions of the North

[In 838, the Norwegians invaded, destroyed almost all the churches, and built castles] in suitable situations all over the country. They were surrounded with deep ditches, and very lofty; being also round, and most of them having three lines of defences. Walled castles, the remains of them, and vestiges of an early age, are to be found to the present day, still entire, but empty and deserted. For the Irish people attach no importance to castles; they make their woods their stronghold, and the bogs their trenches. After this, Turgesius governed the Irish kingdom in peace for some time; until at last he fell into snare laid for him by girls [young men dressed as girls, see Ch. XL], and lost his life.

Source: Giraldus Cambrensis (Gerald of Wales). *The Historical Works of Giraldus Cambrensis. Containing the Topography of Ireland, and the History of the Conquest of Ireland, translated by Thomas Forester. The Itinerary through Wales, and The Description of Wales, translated by Richard Colt Hoare.* Revised and edited by Thomas Wright. London: H. G. Bohn, 1863. The Topography of Ireland, Ch. XL, p. 151.

DOCUMENT 4
The Irish Win through a Daring Trick; They Enter the Castle and Kill the Lord

Turgesius being at that time deeply enamoured of the daughter of Omachlachlelin, king of Meath, the king, disassembling his vindictive feelings, promised to give him his daughter, and to send her to a certain island in Meath, in the lake called Lochyrenus, attended by fifteen damsels of high rank. Turgesius, being highly pleased at this, went to meet them at the appointed day and place, accompanied by the same number of the nobles of his own nation. On his arrival in the island, he was met by fifteen courageous, but beardless youths, who had been selected for the enterprise, and were dressed as young women, with daggers secreted under their mantles; and as soon as Turgesius and his companions advanced to embrace them, they fell upon them and slew them.

Source: Giraldus Cambrensis. *The Topography of Ireland.* Ch. XL, p. 151.

DESCRIPTIONS OF CASTLES

DOCUMENT 5
Gerald Describes His Home, the Castle of Manorbeer

The castle called Maenor Pyrr [Manorbeer] . . . is distant about three miles from Penbroch. It is excellently well defended by turrets and bulwarks, and is situated on the summit of a hill extending on the western side towards the sea-port, having on the northern and southern sides a fine fish-pond under its walls, as conspicuous for its grand appearance, as for the depth of its waters, and a beautiful orchard on the same side, inclosed on one part by a vineyard, and on the other by a wood, remarkable for the projection of rocks, and the height of its hazel trees. On the right hand of the promontory, between the castle and the church, near the site of a very large lake and mill, a rivulet of never-failing water flows through the valley, rendered sandy by the violence of the winds. Towards the west, the Severn sea, bending its course to Ireland, enters a hollow bay at some distance from the castle; and the southern rocks, if extended a little further towards the north, would render it a most excellent harbour for shipping. From this point of sight, you will see almost all the ships of Great Britain, which the east wind drives upon the Irish coast, daringly brave the inconstant waves and raging sea. This country is well supplied with corn, sea-fish, and imported wines; and what is preferable to every other advantage, from its vicinity to Ireland, it is tempered by a salubrious air. Demetia, therefore, with its seven cantreds, is the most beautiful, as well as the most powerful district of Wales: Penbroch, the finest part of the province of Demetia; and the place I have just described, the most beautiful part of Penbroch. It is evident, therefore, that Meanor Pirr is the pleasantest spot in Wales; and the author may be pardoned for having thus extolled his native soil, his genial territory, with a profusion of praise and admiration.

Source: Giraldus Cambrensis. *The Topography of Ireland*. Ch. XII, pp. 406–8.

DOCUMENT 6
The Castle of Ardre, a Huge Timber Castle, Built after Arnold's Return from the First Crusade

Arnold, lord of Ardre . . . built a wooden dwelling upon the dune at Ardre, wondrously put together by carpenters, which in material excelled all the dwellings in Flanders at that time. This an architect or carpenter of Bourbourg named Lodoic planned and constructed, showing himself in this art little worse than Dedalus, and he made and built an almost inextricable labyrinth to receive provisions, with arched vaults, ending at divers places, near to granary or cellars, in a convenient place at the east of the house with a chapel built above it. There were three stories so that like the sun it appeared to be suspended in air. The first floor was a spacious place where were the cellars and granaries, great woven baskets, wide-mouthed jars, and barrels and other domestic utensils. The second floor contained the living quarters and meeting places of the inhabitants in which provisions were, pantries, cupboards, the great bed-chamber of the lord and his wife, near to which was a lavatory and servants rooms, and the room or dormitory for the boys. Here was in a concealed part of the great room a place where one might have a fire for private diversions, morning or evening prayer, or in sickness, or for blood-letting, or for the servants or the little boys. On this floor was joined the kitchens of the lord, on two levels; on the lower pigs were roasted, geese, capons, and other birds killed and prepared for eating. On the other floor of the kitchens other provisions cooked, and here were prepared most delicious viands for the lord, by the means of many cooking vessels, and by laborious rubbing prepared for eating. There the food of the household and servants was also prepared daily from provisions with great labor. On the upper floor of the house were different rooms, which the boys occupied when they desired, or the daughters of the lord (when it was necessary), likewise the watches and servants appointed to the care of the house, while in constant attendance, took what sleep they could there; thus gradually and by little passages it is possible to go from floor to floor, from the living-room into reception hall, which well and sensibly is called logia (where they were accustomed to sit down for conversation) which means "to speak", likewise the logia in an oratory or chapel; like the pictured tabernacle of Solomon. This we call to your memory, oh father and lord, concerning this house which you see, in which you reside, not so much before and on account of you but for the others here assembled. Nor is it strange if the guests or strangers do not realize all the advantages of this dwelling, since many brought up from infancy in this house and grown to manhood may not be able to know and comprehend the number of gates, doors, little doors, and windows.

Source: Lambert, cure of Ardre. *The Chronicle of Guines and of Ardre*. Translated by Majel Irene Kurrie. Master's thesis, University of Chicago, 1925. Ch. CXXVII, pp. 101–3.

DOCUMENT 7
The Masonry Castle at Guines

Afterward Count Baldwin built at his castle in Guines a round tower of hewn stone, high in air, which was level on top, so that an enclosure of lead on rafter and crossbeams superimposed sat on top of the edifice, and from below was not visible because of its height. In this building were built vaults, living-rooms, wardrobes [garderobes], and divers and many kinds of chambers, so that it was like a labyrinth, the home of Dedalus. Before the door of this Count Baldwin built a chapel with alternate layers of wood and stone to the glory of Salomaniaca. In truth, he commenced to enclose the village of Guines by a wall and to make towers at the gates so that it might be protected as well as decorated.

Source: Lambert, cure of Ardre. *The Chronicle of Guines and of Ardre*. Ch. LXXVI, pp. 53–54.

DOCUMENT 8
Repairs and Improvements—Building a Prison, a Chapel, Lists between the Walls, and a Fish Pond

After these things Count Baldwin repaired a tower at the castle of Tornehen which his predecessors had built, but which was damaged by great age, and had so many breaches that scarcely one stone lay on another. And he so repaired and renovated it that it seemed new and entirely different from what it had been before. Also Baldwin made this tower-like structure a labyrinth because of rising galleries, chamber upon chamber, vaults, rooms, and secret places, like the river Meander. Also in the foundation of the tower he dug a secret dungeon, prison-like place infernal, in order to frighten the wicked as well as punish them. In this prison the poor criminals awaited their horrible judgment and in chains with vermin ate the bread of sorrow, and lived in great misery and regret. And at the exit of the tower was made a vault of stone, where was a chapel in which he placed a canon named Siger and to him gave over it in charge. The walls, however, around which often conflicting pugulists and athletes often were seen, he rebuilt and fortified, sharpened, and roughened. A ditch most firm and secure, around part of the church, surrounded and protected the estate; and to the western side the waters of the river Reveria were dammed in their course by earth and stone with great labor and expense, so that it made a great fishpond.

Source: Lambert, cure of Ardre. *The Chronicle of Guines and of Ardre.* Ch. LXXVII, pp. 54–55.

DOCUMENT 9
The Problems of a Medieval Baker when the Oven Is Badly Located

An oven had been built outside the fortifications between the castle gate and the assailant's belfry, and there the baker baked the bread required for the use of the garrison, because the siege was begun in haste that they had no time to construct an oven within their defense. It followed therefore that the thickest of the fight often raged around this oven, much blood was shed there, and many spirits departed by violence from the prison of the flesh. For the people of Courci stood in arms to defend their bread, while Belèsme's followers tried to carry it off, so that many desperate conflicts occurred. It happened that one day while the loaves were being baked in the oven, and the two hostile parties were engaged in a violent quarrel, the troops on both sides came up, and a desperate conflict ensued, in which twenty men were killed and more wounded, who never tasted the bread their blood had purchased.

Source: Ordericus Vitalis. *The Ecclesiastical History of England and Normandy by Ordericus Vitalis.* Translated by Thomas Forester. London: Henry G. Bohn, 1856. Bk. VI, Ch. XVI, p. 509.

DOCUMENT 10
Separate Bedrooms but a Convenient Spiral Staircase in a Thirteenth-Century Castle

The unkindness that Queen Blanche [the French king's mother], showed to the Queen Margaret was such that she would not suffer, in so far as she could help it, that her son [Louis IX], should be in his wife's company, except at night when he went to sleep with her. The palace where the king and queen liked most to dwell was at Pontoise, because there the king's chamber was above and the queen's chamber below; and they had so arranged matters between them that they held their converse [met] in a turning staircase that went from the one chamber to the other; and they had further arranged that when the ushers saw Queen Blanche coming to her son's chamber, they struck the door with their rods, and the king would come running into his chamber so that his mother might find him there; and the ushers of Queen Margaret's chamber did the same when Queen Blanche went thither, so that she might find Queen Margaret there.

Source: Jean de Joinville. *Chronicles of the Crusades by Villehardouin and De Joinville.* Translated by Sir Frank Marzials. London: J. M. Dent; New York: E. P. Dutton, 1908. P. 166.

DOCUMENT 11
A Crusader's Sorrow at Leaving Home

And never while I [the lord of Joinville] went to Blécourt and Saint-Urbain would I turn my eyes toward Joinville for fear my heart would melt within me at thought of the fair castle I was leaving behind, and my two children.

Source: Jean de Joinville. *Chronicles of the Crusades of St. Louis.* P. 166.

BUILDING THE CASTLE

DOCUMENT 12
The Mound Is Built

The building of a mound for a castle at Ardre, replacing the older town of Selnesse Arnold when he saw that fortune favored him and everything he desired came about, began to build in the little marsh at Ardre two different buildings near the mill, about a stone's throw apart. Between which in the midst of the mud of the marsh, at its most profound depth, near the foot of a mountain, he had raised a high mound, or dike of earth, as a sort of fortification, and he accumulated a great mass. So around this another wall, enclosing the interior mound, made a most firm fortification. Later as his father had planned he tore down and destroyed all his buildings at Selnesse and built on the dune at Ardre a bridge, gate, and the necessary buildings. And so today Selnesse with its castle is forgotten, the great place spoiled and the buildings torn down, and the new buildings carried to and built at Ardre; so that Arnold should be called the protector and lord of Ardre.

Source: Lambert, cure of Ardre. *The Chronicle of Guines and of Ardre.* Ch. CIX, p. 90.

DOCUMENT 13
The Castle and the Master Builder

. . . Arnold of Guines [d. 1220] saw all the castles and fortifications and provisions had been cared for and made stronger by the advice of his father and the peers and townspeople of the town of Ardre he included and surrounded by a most safe ditch like that of St. Omer, such as never before had been attempted or had an eye seen in the land of Guines, his own Ardre situated in the center and middle of the land of Guines which had grown to be more rich than the other castles and towns of Guines and an object of envy to its ravaging adversaries, and because of this greater value ought to be preserved carefully. There were moreover not a few workers at the making and digging of the aforementioned ditch afflicted rather by the violence of the times and the great famine rather than by the labor of the day and the heat of the summer; the workers stifled their hunger and alleviated much labor talking and joking together. Many moreover came for the cause of seeing such a great ditch. Paupers, indeed, who were not among the workers, in the pleasure of seeing the work did not remember their poverty. In truth, many knights and townsmen and presbyters and monks came not only one day but often to marvel at the sight. Who in truth unless lazy and overwhelmed with age or worry did not delight to see Simon master of the ditch, skilled in the geometry of the work, proceeding with his customary wand of office, and having already in his mind the finished plan, not so much using his rod as his staff for the eyes, and destroying houses and barns, cutting down apple trees and trees flourishing and bearing fruit, seeing commons ruined which had been prepared with the greatest zeal and labor for the enjoyment of all on feast days, excavating gardens fragrant and sweet-smelling, crops trampled and destroyed to make passage, notwithstanding the indignation, tears, and silent curses of many toward him? Moreover these same peasants with wagons for sod, dung wagons for bearing stones for spreading in the road, entertained themselves alternately working in gloves of hide and in working jacket. These ditch-diggers with digging tools, spaders with spades, pickaxe men with picks, hammerers with paving rams, hewers with material to clear the soil, also men to line and make walls, and deuparii [translation unknown] and rammers with the convenient and necessary instruments and armaments, loaders also and hod carriers with baskets and sodders who worked with the turf and rampart builders at the wish of the magistrates in the meadow with implements for cutting and tearing up; the serving people moreover and sergeants with rods and pointed sticks, the workers worked alternately inspired, alternately being worked, proceeded always be the plan of the masters adhering strictly to geometry. And the workers were struck and tormented in the work and in the toil never ceasing, always in labor and toil and in anguish and pain.

Source: Lambert, cure of Ardre. *The Chronicle of Guines and of Ardre.* Ch. CLII, pp. 118–20.

DOCUMENT 14
The Crew Needed to Build a Castle, and the Hazards They Faced

Baldwin had built a fine fortress at Sangatte arousing the envy of Regnault.

And when Regnault, Count of Boulogne saw this tower built at Sangatte, and when Baldwin Count of Guines and his men held the garrison there, and in this triumphed in making banquets and good cheer more than at any other place, and as he feared for himself and his country, his ire and indignation arose, and he gathered all his men of arms and people of Ostruicq near the fortress of Sangatte at the place of the stinking Sliviacas, in order to destroy and lay low the name and fortress of Sangatte, by constructing if possible a rival castle. Here he collected ditch diggers, wood workers, burden bearers, and ox drivers, and other workers, and architects of castles and ditches, assisted by men at arms and the principal men of his country, and the earth was raised into a mound, and around this a ditch dug for defense. Which those of Guines and Sangatte perceiving, being brave men and war-like, they were full of indignation and gave vent to their anger by giving mortal wounds by their archers and crossbowmen, and rushing upon those workmen of their adversary on all sides, setting in flight the chief men and the soldiers, who left the work unfinished after much loss of blood, where it lies today. And this is the situation at Sangatte so that even though of age the castle and its foundations are gone, the memory is not lost, but endures forever.

Source: Lambert, cure of Ardre. *The Chronicle of Guines and of Ardre.* Ch. LXXXIV, p. 62.

DOCUMENT 15
Compulsory Service on Castle Building and Destruction

The count de Belèsme [Robert who owned thirty-four castles] urged forward the demolition of the new castle, with all his influence, employing the peasants from all his own lordships and the neighbourhood in the compulsory duty of working at its destruction. The vassals of Evreux took no part in the labour, because they owed no service to the count, upon which he was greatly incensed with the monks, and did them great injuries for a whole year. He compelled by violence the tenants of St. Evroult to work at the fortifications of his own castle, carrying off the goods of those who shrunk from the labour; and he even threatened to lay the abbey in ruins, unless they submitted to his will in all things as their lord.

Source: Ordericus Vitalis. *The Ecclesiastical History of England and Normandy*. Bk. VIII, Ch. XXIV, p. 29.

DOCUMENT 16
The Burden of Castle Building on the People, 1066

And Bishop Odo [Bishop of Bayeux] and William the earl [William Fitz Osburn, Earl of Hereford] remained here behind, and built castles wide throughout the nation, and poor people distressed; and ever after it greatly grew in evil.

Source: *The Anglo-Saxon Chronicle*. Translated by Rev. James Ingram. London: J. M. Dent; New York: E. P. Dutton, 1913. P. 442.

DOCUMENT 17
The Burden of Castle Building on the People, 1087

Truly there was much trouble in these times, and very great distress; he [William the Conqueror] caused castles to be built, and oppressed the poor.

Source: *The Anglo-Saxon Chronicle*. P. 462.

DOCUMENT 18
The Common People Hated the Castles

1137

When king Stephen came to England, he held an assembly at Oxford; and there he seized Roger bishop of Salisbury, and Alexander bishop of Lincoln, and Robert the chancellor, his nephew, and he kept them all in prison till they gave up their castles. . . . [A]ll became forsworn, and broke their allegiance, for every rich man built his castles, and defended them against him, and they filled the land full of castles. They greatly oppressed the wretched people by making them work at these castles, and when the castles were finished they filled them with devils and evil men.

Source: *The Anglo-Saxon Chronicle.* Pp. 502–3.

DOCUMENT 19
A Demand for Wages in the Fourteenth Century

It is customary in England, as well as in several other countries, for the nobility to have the greatest advantages over the commonality; that is to say, the lower orders are bound by law to plough the lands of the gentry, to harvest their grain, to carry it home to the barn, to thrash and winnow it; they are also bound to harvest and carry home the hay. All these services the prelates and gentlemen exact of their inferiors; . . . [People] began to murmur, saying, that in the beginning of the world there were no slaves, and that no one ought to be treated as such, unless he had committed treason against the lord, as Lucifer had against God; but they had done no such thing, for they were neither angels nor spirits, but men formed after the likeness of these lords who treated them as beasts. This they would bear no longer; they were determined to be free, and if they laboured or did any work, they would be paid for it.

Source: Jean Froissart. *The Chronicles of England, France, and Spain by Sir John Froissart.* Translated by Thomas Johnes. New York: The Colonial Press, c. 1901; London: J. M. Dent; New York: E. P. Dutton, 1906. P. 207.

THE CASTLE AT WAR

DOCUMENT 20
The Norman Conquest of England

The duke [William the Conqueror] then continued his march to Dover, where there was a large body of people collected, because they thought the position impregnable, the castle standing on a steep rock, overhanging the sea. The garrison, however, struck with panic at the duke's approach, were preparing to surrender, when some Norman squires, greedy for spoil, set the place on fire, and the devouring flames spreading around, many parts were ruined or burnt. The duke, compassionating [sic] those who were willing to render him their submission, ordered them to be paid the cost of rebuilding their houses, and their other losses. The castle being taken, eight days were spent strengthening the fortifications. While he lay there a great number of soldiers, who devoured flesh-meat half raw and drank too much water, died of dysentery.

Source: Ordericus Vitalis. *The Ecclesiastical History of England and Normandy.* Bk. III, Ch. XIV, p. 488.

DOCUMENT 21
The Failure of an Attack on Dover Castle

But while the assailants made desperate attacks upon the place [Dover Castle], the garrison were prepared for an obstinate defense, and offered a determined resistance at the points most open to attack. The conflict was maintained with fury on both sides for some hours of the day. But Eustace [Count of Boulogne] beginning to be doubtful of success, and being apprehensive of a sally by the besieged, which might force him to a more shameful retreat, gave the signal for retiring the ships. Upon this the garrison immediately opened the gates and falling on the rear guard with spirit, but in good order, killed a great many of them. The fugitives, panic struck by a report that the bishop of Bayeux had unexpectedly arrived with a strong force, threw themselves with their alarm among the crevices of the perpendicular cliffs, and so perished with more disgrace than if they had fallen by the sword. Many were the forms of death to which their defeat exposed them, many, throwing away their arms, were killed by falling on the sharp rocks; others, slipping down, destroyed themselves and their comrades by their own weapons; and many, mortally wounded, or bruised by their fall, rolled yet breathing into the sea; many more, escaping breathless with haste to the ships, were so eager to reach a place of safety that they crowded the vessels till they upset them and were drowned on the spot. The Norman cavalry took prisoners or slew as many as they could overtake. Eustace escaped by having the advantage of a fleet horse, his knowledge of the road, and finding a ship ready to put to sea. His nephew, a noble youth who bore arms for the first time, was taken prisoner. The English escaped through the by-roads, the garrison of the castle being too few in number to pursue a multitude who thus dispersed themselves.

Source: Ordericus Vitalis. *The Ecclesiastical History of England and Normandy.* Bk. IV, Ch. III, pp. 11–12.

DOCUMENT 22
The Siege of Rochester and the Plague of Flies, 1088

Upon this, Odo, bishop of Bayeux, shut himself up in the city of Rochester with five hundred men of arms, determining to wait for the arrival of Duke Robert with the auxiliary forces he had promised to bring; for the league, although they were very numerous and had great resources in money and arms, and vast supplies, did not dare to meet the king in open fight within his own realm. They therefore, with great prudence, selected Rochester, because if the king did not blockade them in the city, the position was central for making sudden eruptions and plundering London and Canterbury, and they could also take advantage of the sea, which lies very near, and the neighboring islands, to dispatch messengers to obtain assistance. The resolute king, however, anticipated their projects, and in the month of May, invested the place with a powerful army; and erecting two forts, shut up the enemy within the walls so that every avenue of egress was closed. As I have said before, Bishop Odo, Count Eustace, and Robert de Belèsme, with many nobles, as well as persons of moderate station, held the place, expecting in vain, succours from Duke Robert, who was detained by sloth and indulgence. However Roger, earl of Mercia, and many other Normans who were in the besieging army gave secret aid to the besieged, as far as it was in their power, although they did not venture to appear openly in arms against the king. All the bishops of England joined the English people in loyally supporting the king, and laboured to restore in the country the tranquility, which good men love. Also Hugh, earl of Chester, Robert de Mowbray, earl of Northumberland, William de Warenne, and Robert Fitz-Hamon, with their loyal and experienced barons, maintained their fealty to their sovereign and gave him useful aid, both with their arms and their counsels, against the enemy.

A plague, like the plague of the Egyptians, made its appearance in the town of Rochester, the Almighty, who, in all ages, superintends human affairs and orders them aright, having chosen to renew an ancient miracle in modern times. For as the flies tormented the Egyptians, and did not cease a moment from whizzing around them, in the same manner these flies grievously annoyed the besieged with their incessant attacks; for all egress from the castle was prevented, and many of those who were thus blockaded fell sick from their various sufferings, and, their disorders increasing, at length died. Innumerable flies were engendered in the dung of men and horses and being nourished by the heat both of the summer, and the atmosphere caused by the breath of so many inhabitants closely pent up, their swarms horribly infested their eyes and noses, food and drink. So severely was the insolent band of rebels afflicted with the annoyance of the swarms that they could not eat their meals, either by day or by night, unless a great number of them were employed, in turn, in flapping them away from their comrades faces. In consequence, Odo and his allies could no longer suffer the miseries of the siege; they therefore sent envoys to the king asking for peace and offering to surrender the place.

Source: Ordericus Vitalis. *The Ecclesiastical History of England and Normandy*. Bk. VIII, Ch. II, pp. 436–38.

DOCUMENT 23
The Rapid and Cowardly Departure of a Castle's Garrison

Paganus de Montdoubleau and Rotrou de Montfort, and some others who were charged with its defense, abandoned the place; and favoring Belèsme as some say, left the castle [Giroie's Castle] without anyone to guard it, though no person molested them. Radegunde, Giroie's wife, turned pale at the fearful rumour [of her husband's death], but determined, while waiting for their confirmation, to remain in the castle with her attendants. What, however, could a lone woman do against stubborn men determined to have their own way. Meanwhile, Robert de Belèsme's attention was attracted by the disorderly shouts of those who were leaving the place, and immediately coming up and finding it deserted by the defenders, he easily forced to an entrance, and, giving up to the pillage, then set fire to it. The assailants found within pots full of meat boiling on the fires, and the tables covered with cloths, and spread with dishes of food. [Radegunde and her son, taken hostage by Robert of Belèsme, died that same year, probably from poison. Giroie eventually got his lordship back, married again, and had three sons and three daughters.]

Source: Ordericus Vitalis. *The Ecclesiastical History of England and Normandy.* Bk. VIII, Ch. XXIV, p. 27.

DOCUMENT 24
The Burning of a City

For Walter, son of Ansger, the commander of the castle, ordered the smiths he employed there to set to work, and caused the burning cinders to be hurled by his engineers on the roofs of the houses. "At that time the sun was blazing in the lofty Gemini," and the earth was burnt up with severe drought. The fiery whirlwind caught the roofs of the houses, and the flames burst out with such violence that the whole city was burnt.

Source: Ordericus Vitalis. *The Ecclesiastical History of England and Normandy.* Bk. IX, Ch. IX, p. 239.

SIEGE ENGINES

DOCUMENT 25
Bohemund's Siege Engines

[Dyrrachium (Durazzio) on the Dalmatian coast] . . . he [Bohemund] was constructing machines of war, building movable sheds (or 'tortoises') with towers and battering rams, and other sheds to protect the diggers and the sappers, he worked all the winter and summer.

Source: Anna Comnena. _The Alexiad of the Princess Anna Comnena._ Translated by Elizabeth A. S. Dawes. London: Kegan Paul, Trench, Trubner, 1928. Bk. XIII, p. 327.

DOCUMENT 26
The Battering Ram

First he completed a tortoise with a battering ram, an indescribable object, and rolled it up to the eastern side of the city. And merely to look at it was a fearsome sight, for it was built in the following manner. They made a small shed, fashioning it in the shape of a parallelogram, put wheels under it, and covered its sides, both above and laterally, with ox-hides sewn together, and thus as Homer would say, they made the roof and walls of the machine 'of seven bull's-hides,' and then hung the battering rams inside. When the machine was ready, he drove it up to the wall by means of a large number of men pushing it along from inside with poles and bringing it close to the walls of Dyrrachium. When it seemed near enough and at an appropriate distance, they took off the wheels, and fixed the machine firmly on all sides with wooden pegs, so that the roof might not be shaken to pieces by the blows. Afterwards some very strong men on either side of the ram pushed it violently against the wall with regular co-ordinated movement. The men would push forward the ram violently with a single movement and the ram thus brought up against the wall shattered it, then it rebounded, and returning made a second shattering. And this it did several times as it was swung several times in either direction, and did not cease making holes in the walls.

Source: Anna Comnena. _The Alexiad._ Bk. XIII, p. 328.

DOCUMENT 27
Mining Operations

The Praetorium stood on a hill, not a hill of rock but earth, and the wall of the city ran over it. Opposite this hill Bohemund's men began to dig in a definite direction. For the besiegers had devised this new mischief against the city and invented a new knavish siege-engine to apply to the town. For as they dug, they went along under the ground like moles boring holes in the soil and in places protecting themselves by sheds with high roofs against the stones and arrows which were thrown from above, and in others propping up the earth above them with poles, and thus they went in a straight line. So they made a very long and broad tunnel and always carried away the earth from their diggings in wagons. When they had bored through sufficiently far, they rejoiced as if they had accomplished a great task. But the men in the city were not negligent for at some distance from the other city dug out earth and made a good-sized tunnel and then posted themselves along its whole strength to watch for the spot where the besieging party would break through from their tunnel to ours. And soon they found it, for they heard them knocking and digging and undermining the base of the walls. . . . Then they opened up a little hole opposite and when they saw the quantity of workers by means of this peep-hole, they burnt their faces to ashes with fire. Now this fire is prepared in the following ingredients. The readily combustible rosin is collected from the pine and other similar evergreen trees and mixed with sulpher. Then it is introduced into reed-pipes and blown by the man using it with a strong continuous breath and at the other end fire is applied to it and bursts into flame and falls like a streak of lightening on the faces of the men opposite. This fire the men of Dyrrachium used directly [as soon as] they were face to face with the enemy, and burnt their beards and faces. And the enemy could be seen, like a swarm of bees which had been smoked out, rushing out in disorder from the place they had entered in good order.

Source: Anna Comnena. *The Alexiad*. Bk. XIII, p. 329.

DOCUMENT 28
The Siege Tower

Bohemund's men also built a wooden tower.

The tower was certainly terrible to look at, and when moving it seemed more terrible. For its base was raised on a number of wheels, and, as it was levered along with crowbars by the soldiers inside, it caused amazement, as the source of its motion was invisible and it seemed to be moving of its own accord like some towering giant. It was completely covered in from top to base and divided into several floors, and all around were openings in the shape of loop-holes through which arrows were shot. On the top floor stood high-spirited men, fully armed, with swords in their hands ready to stand on defence. When this terrific object drew near the wall, the men under Alexius, the military governor of the city of Dyrrachium, lost no time, but whilst Bohemund was building this machine outside the walls, to be an infallible captor of the city, they built a counter one inside. For seeing to what a height that self-moving tower reached and where they had planted it after taking off the wheels, they fixed opposite the tower four very long beams which stood up like scaffolding from a square base. Then they introduced some flooring between these upright beams and thus made an erection which exceeded the wooden tower outside by one cubit. And the structure was left open all round for it did not require any protection except at the top where it was roofed over. Next Alexius' soldiers carried up the liquid fire to the top story of the open structure with intent to shoot it against the wooden tower opposite. But this idea and its execution did not seem sufficient for the complete destruction of the machine. For the fire when directed against it would only catch the extreme top of the tower. So what did they devise? They filled the space between the wooden tower and the city tower with all kinds of flammable material and poured streams of oil upon it. To this they applied fire, namely torches and fire-brands, which smoldered for a short time, then flared up a little and finally burst into tall flames. As the fiery streaks of the liquid fire also contributed their share, that whole terrific construction all made of wood caught fire, and made an immense noise and was a terrible sight for the eyes. And that enormous fire was seen for thirteen stades round. The tumult and confusion of the barbarians inside was tremendous and hopeless, for some were caught by the fire and burnt to ashes, and others threw themselves to the ground from the top. And there was also much shouting and wild confusion among the barbarians outside who re-echoed their cries.

Source: Anna Comnena. *The Alexiad.* Bk. XIII, pp. 330–31.

THE SIEGE OF JERUSALEM

DOCUMENT 29
The Assault

On Monday the crusaders made a vigorous assault on the city, and it was believed they would have taken it if they had been sufficiently supplied with scaling ladders. They made a breach of the outer wall, and raised one ladder against the inner one. The Christian knights mounted it by turns and fought with the Saracens on the battlements hand to hand with swords and lances. In these assaults many fell on both sides, but most on the side of the Gentiles. [Another account tells us that the crusaders had only one ladder. The first man to climb it reached the top, and as he grasped the battlement the defenders chopped his hand off and he fell back to his companions. He survived and was rewarded with a piece of the True Cross, which he took back home to France.] The trumpets sounding the recall, the Christians at length withdrew from the combat, and returned to their camps. Meanwhile, the provisions they brought with them began to fail, nor could bread be purchased for money, nor was any one able to succeed in foraging. The country round is entirely without water, and is moreover arid and rocky, affording no pasture for the subsistence of beasts of burden or other animals. It is also naked of trees and therefore produces but little fruit; bearing only olive and palm, with a few vines.

Source: Ordericus Vitalis. *The Ecclesiastical History of England and Normandy.* Bk. IX, Ch. XV, p. 171.

DOCUMENT 30
Difficulties for Those Conducting a Siege

Meanwhile, the Christians employed in the siege were suffering the torments of constant thirst. The Pagans lay in ambush for the people who had to drive the horses six miles to water, and occasioned them great losses in the narrow defiles. Cedron and the other torrents were dried up by the excessive drought. Even barley-bread was dear in the camp. The natives, concealing themselves in dens and caverns, interrupted all conveys of provisions.

The chiefs of the army assembled in council to consider what was to be done in the midst of the calamities. They said, "We are in difficulties on all sides; bread is wanting; the water has failed. We ourselves are, in fact, closely blockaded, while we fancy we are besieging the city. We can hardly venture outside our camp, and when we do, return empty. Our long delays have produced the scarcity, and, unless we find a remedy matters will become worse. This place can never be taken by the mere strength of our hands and arms without the engines of war. We have to contend against the walls and bulwarks, and towers; we are opposed by a numerous garrison who make an obstinate defence. What then is your opinion? Let us undertake something which will relieve ourselves and distress the besieged. We want timber to construct machines for assaulting the walls and towers of the place. As the country is not woody, let us take the rafters of the houses and beams from the churches, and shape them to our purpose, so that we may attack the city in the most determined manner; otherwise, we waste our time to nor purpose."

At length the faithful champions of the cross discovered some timber at a great distance from the camp, to which they transported it with vast labour. Carpenters were assembled from the whole army, some of whom hewed the rough surface of the trees, others squared it and bored it, while the rest fitted the beams and planks together. Duke Godfrey built one machine at his own expense; the count of Tholouse caused another to be constructed at his proper cost. On the other hand, the Saracens used every effort to strengthen the fortifications, raising the towers higher by working in the night, and devoting themselves without respite to increase the defences.

One Saturday, Duke Godfrey's machine was transported in the dead of night to the foot of the walls, and erected before sunrise, three days being employed in unremitting exertions to fit the parts together and prepare it for use. The count of Tholouse caused his machine, which might be called a castle of wood, to be placed near the wall on the south of the place, but a deep hollow prevented its being joined to the wall. Such machines cannot be guided on declivities nor carried up steep places, and can only be transported on level ground. Proclamation was therefore made through the camp that whoever should cast three stones into the hole should for so doing receive a penny. In consequence all the people who were weary of delay lent a hand willingly to the proposed work.

Source: Ordericus Vitalis. *The Ecclesiastical History of England and Normandy.* Bk. IX, Ch. XV, pp. 173–75.

DOCUMENT 31
The Assault on Jerusalem

Duke Godfrey and his brother Eustace fought bravely at the head of the troops, and the rest followed their lead. Then Letold and Rambold Croton, two brave soldiers, mounted the walls, and uttering loud cries, continued to struggle without giving way. They were followed by several others, and those who had hitherto defended the fortifications fled on all sides, and no longer thought of the defence of the city. Crowds of Christians rushed in, and pursuing the fugitives gave no quarter.

Source: Ordericus Vitalis. *The Ecclesiastical History of England and Normandy.* Bk. IX, Ch. XV, p. 177.

DOCUMENT 32
The Massacre of the People of Jerusalem

The dispersed citizens again collected, and made a stand in the temple of Solomon, where they resisted stoutly the attacks of the Christians, but being at last driven to despair, they laid down their arms and submitted to their fate. No one knows the number of the slain, but the floor of the temple was knee deep in blood, and great heaps of corpses were piled up in all quarters of the city, as the victors spared neither age, sex, rank, nor condition of any kind. . . . But it profited them little or nothing, for not even these were spared by the Christians, except that they suffered some few to live that they might employ them in burying the dead; but these were afterwards butchered or sold as slaves. . . . The victors did not pillage and set fire to the city like other places taken by storm, but finding the houses well supplied with all the conveniences, they reserved them for their own use, and many liberally shared with the poor the stores they found. Each one quietly appropriated the first house he came to, whether it was large or small, deserted by the Pagans, and take free possession of it with all the wealth it contained, preserves it as a heritage to the present day.

The crusaders, having thus at length secured their triumph, hastened in crowds to cover with kisses the tomb of their blessed Saviour, having first cleansed their hands from the stain of blood; and many of them approaching it with bare feet and tears of joy, offered their thanksgivings and sacrifices of peace. The faithful indulged in transports of joy, now that they had gained the object of their long cherished hopes, which they had sought through so many toils and dangers. They now witnessed with delight the end of their labours, and being secure for the present formed exalted conceptions of their future recompense. However their immediate attention was called to the necessity of clearing the city of the bodies of the slain, for the spectacle was horrid and the stench insupportable. The corpses were therefore piled in heaps by the captive Gentiles and the poorer pilgrims who were paid for the service, and being burnt, the city was thus freed from impurities.

Source: Ordericus Vitalis. *The Ecclesiastical History of England and Normandy*. Bk. IX, Ch. XV, pp. 180–81.

THE SUCCESSFUL ATTACK AND THE SURRENDER OF THE CASTLE

DOCUMENT 33
The Water Supply Is Cut at Alencon

Thenceforth he [the Count of Anjou] pressed the siege [of Alencon] with more security, and cut off the supply of water and subterranean works, secretly carried on; for the inhabitants were well acquainted with the conduit by which the founders of the citadel introduced the water of the Sarthe into the place. The troops [of King Henry I] shut up in the fortress finding their provisions fail, and that no relief arrived from any quarter, submitted, and surrendering the citadel, marched out under safe conduct with all their baggage. These disasters gave occasion to much pillage, and the season of our Lord's Advent was little observed.

Source: Ordericus Vitalis. *The Ecclesiastical History of England and Normandy*. Bk. XII, Ch. VIII, p. 463.

DOCUMENT 34
The Countess Surrenders the Castles

1095

And he [King William Rufus] besieged Tinmouth castle until he took it, and there he seized the earl's brother, and all who were with him: thence he proceeded to Bambrough, and there besieged the earl [Robert, Earl of Northumberland]; and when the king found that he could not re-duce [destroy] him, he caused the castle to be built over against Bam-brough, and called it in his speech Malveisin, which is in English "the evil neighbour," and he garrisoned it strongly, and afterwards departed southward. Then one night, soon after the king's return to the south, the earl went out of Bambrough towards Tinmouth: but those in the new cas-tle, being aware of his design, pursued and attacked him, and they wounded him, and afterwards took him prisoner, and some of his fol-lowers were slain, and some taken alive. . . . When the king came back, he commanded his people to take Robert earl of Northumberland, and lead him to Bambrough, and to put out both his eyes, unless the besieged, would surrender the castle, which was defended by his wife, and his stew-ard Morel, who was also his kinsman. On this, the castle was given up, and Morel was received at William's court.

Source: *The Anglo-Saxon Chronicle*. Pp. 472–73.

DOCUMENT 35
The Siege of Brevol; Returning Crusaders Bring Experience back to Europe

The priests, with their parishioners, brought their banners, and the abbots assembling their vassals joined the besieging army. At the same time Robert de Belèsme furnished a most ingenious machine such as his talent for engineering had invented at the siege of Jerusalem. He caused engines to be built which were impelled on wheels against the enemy's fortification, he hurled vast stones as projectiles into the besieged place and among the garrison, instructed the besiegers in making assaults so as to destroy the trenches and palisades surrounding the fortress, and to shatter the roofs of the houses upon the inhabitants, until overwhelmed with calamities, the enemy should be forced to surrender.

Source: Ordericus Vitalis. *The Ecclesiastical History of England and Normandy.* Bk. VIII, Ch. XXIV, p. 24.

DOCUMENT 36
The Surrender of Rochester Castle, the Trumpets Sound

In consequence, the noble minded king, vanquished by the prayers of his faithful followers, granted their request, and relieving the besieged from the sentence of death or mutilation, granted them leave to depart from the place with their horses and arms. But he utterly refused them all expectation of having any inheritance or lands within the realm of England, as long as he was on the throne. Then Bishop Odo attempted to procure the king's command that the trumpeters should not sound a flourish while the garrison moved out, as is the custom when any enemy is conquered, and a fortress is taken by storm. But the king fell into a great passion, and would not listen to what was asked, asserting that he would not grant it for a thousand marks of gold. The garrison therefore marched out with sorrow and dejection, while the royal trumpets sounded in notes of triumph, and the crowds of English who were on the king's side shouted aloud, "Halters, bring halters, and hang the traitor-bishop with his accomplices on a gallows."

Source: Ordericus Vitalis. *The Ecclesiastical History of England and Normandy.* Bk.VIII, Ch. II, pp. 440–41.

DOCUMENT 37
The Ice Torture of Prisoners and the High Cost of Freedom

In the month of February [1092], Ascelin . . . engaging in battle with William, his lord . . . defeated him and made him captive, putting his troops to flight with the loss of some who were taken prisoners. Elated with this victory, he became exceedingly arrogant, and cruelly tormented his lord and Roger de Glos and his other captives. He kept them in close confinement in his castle of Breval for three months, and often in the severest weather, during winter, exposed them in their shirts, well soaked in water, at a window in the highest stage of the tower to the blasts of the north or south winds, until their only covering was frozen into a sheet of ice round their bodies. At length, by the interference of friends, peace was concluded between them, and William was let out of prison on these conditions: he gave his daughter Isabel in marriage to Goel, and delivered to him three thousand livres, with horses and arms and many other things, promising to surrender the castle of Ivri. On these terms William was liberated; but the peace was of short duration.

Source: Ordericus Vitalis. *The Ecclesiastical History of England and Normandy.* Bk. VIII, Ch. XXIV, p. 23.

THE SUCCESSFUL DEFENSE OF THE CASTLE

DOCUMENT 38
A Successful Defense

Count Elias [who opposed William Rufus] remained at Château-du-Loir with a considerable number of troops, and reserving himself for better times, waited the course of events. At least on Friday, the king sat down before Maiet [south of Mans], and ordered his troops to storm the castle the following day. But when Saturday came, and the soldiers were busy in putting on their armour, and preparing to make a vigorous assault on the garrison, the king, by the advice of his counselors and for the glory of God, spared the enemy out of respect to the day of the Lord's burial and resurrection, granting them a truce until Monday. The besieged took advantage of the interval to strengthen their defences, and to weaken the force of the bolts and stones hurled against them with a quantity of wicker baskets. They were resolute men, faithful to their lord, and determined to fight for him to the last extremity, so that their merit deserves commendation. The assailants had by excessive toil filled up the ditch surrounding the fortifications with great heaps of wood, and were openly engaged in making a road to the foot of the palisades supported by immense beams, when the garrison threw down vessels full of burning coals, and set fire to the heaps of combustible matter which had been collected for their injury, and, assisted by the summer heat, speedily reduced them to ashes. Both sides suffered very much in this assault, which took place on Monday, so that the king who was witness of it was much distressed. While he was tormented with rage and vexation because all his efforts to reduce the place proved fruitless, one of the garrison hurled a stone at him from the top of a turret, which by God's mercy did not strike the king, but crushed the head of the soldier standing near him, so that his brains were mingled with his fractured skull. As he thus miserably perished in the king's presence, the sounds of scornful laughter were heard from the garrison, who raised the loud and horrible cry: "There is fresh meat for the king; take it to the kitchen to be cooked for his supper."

Source: Ordericus Vitalis. *The Ecclesiastical History of England and Normandy*. Bk. X, Ch. XV, pp. 242–43.

DOCUMENT 39
The Siege Tower, Called a Belfry, at the Siege of Courci

In the year, therefore, of our Lord 1091, the thirteenth indiction, in the month of January, the duke laid siege to Courci, but unwilling to come to extremities with his great nobles, he took no measures for closely investing the besieged. Robert, however, used every resource of open attack and stratagem against the enemy for three weeks, employing various engines of war in his assaults on the fortress; but the garrison being numerous and making resolute defense, he was repulsed with shame. He caused a vast machine, called a belfry, to be erected over against the castle walls, and filled it with all kinds of war-like instruments, but even this failed of compelling the garrison to submit; for as often as he began an assault on Courci, the powerful force from Grantmesnil hastened to the rescue, and charging the assailants with fury drew them off from their intended attack.

Source: Ordericus Vitalis. *The Ecclesiastical History of England and Normandy*. Bk. VIII, Ch. XVI, pp. 507–8.

DOCUMENT 40
A Constable Saves His Castle by Pretending to Have Plenty of Food

Arnulph de Montgomery, in the reign of king Henry I, erected here a slender fortress with stakes and turf, which, on returning to England, he consigned to the care of Giraldus de Windesor, his constable and lieutenant-general, a worthy and discreet man. . . . [T]he inhabitants of South Wales besieged the castle. One night, when fifteen soldiers had deserted, and endeavored to escape from the castle in a small boat, on the following morning Giraldus invested their armour bearers with the arms and estates of their masters, and decorated them with the military order. The garrison being, from the length of the siege, reduced to the utmost want of provisions, the constable, with great prudence and flattering hopes of success, caused four hogs, which yet remained, to be cut into small pieces and thrown down to the enemy from the fortifications. The next day, having again recourse to a more refined stratagem, he contrived that a letter, sealed with his own signet, should be found before the house of Wilfred, bishop of St. David's, who was then by chance in that neighbourhood, as if accidentally dropped, stating that there would be no necessity of soliciting the assistance of Earl Arnulph for the next four months to come. The contents of these letters being made known to the army, the troops abandoned the siege of the castle, and retired to their own homes.

Source: Giraldus Cambrensis. *The Itinerary through Wales*. Bk. XII, p. 405.

DOCUMENT 41
The Escape of the Bishop of Durham from the Tower of London

Ranulph Flambard, bishop of Durham, was the chief instigator of this mad enterprise [giving the duchy of Normandy to the king of England]. He was a man of low origin, who, by his flatteries and crafty policy, had so crept into the favor of William Rufus, that he was raised by that king above all nobles of the realm. Being made lord high treasurer and justiciary, he brought on himself the hatred and fear of numbers of the king's subjects, by the cruel severities with which he performed his functions. Amassing wealth and enlarging his property in all quarters, he became enormously rich, and was advanced to the episcopacy, although he was illiterate, not for his piety, but for his worldly power. But as all earthly prosperity is of short duration, on the death of his patron, King William, the bishop was thrown into prison by the new king as an inveterate robber of his country. For the many injuries he had inflicted on Henry [Henry I] himself and the other children of the soil, both rich and poor, by which he had in various ways heaped constant troubles upon them, he was, thanks to divine providence which changed the current of affairs, hurled from his proud elevation, and committed to the custody of William de Magnaville, to be confined in fetters in the tower of London. . . .

. . . [T]he crafty prelate contrived his release from prison, effecting his liberation by the adroit use of his friend's assistance. Indeed, he had great ability and fluency of speech, and although he was cruel and passionate, such was his generosity and constant good humour, that he rendered himself a general favorite, and was even beloved. By the king's command, he was allowed every day two shillings for his diet in confinement, so that with the assistance of his friends, he fared sumptuously for a prisoner, and kept daily a splendid table for himself and his keepers. One day [in February 1101] a cord was brought to the bishop in a flagon of wine, and, causing a plentiful banquet to be served, the guards having partaken of it in his company, washed it down with Falernian cups in the highest spirits. Having intoxicated them to such a degree that they slept soundly, the bishop secured a cord to the mullion in the center of the tower window, and, catching up his pastoral staff, began to lower himself by means of the cord. But now, having forgotten to put on gloves, his hands were excoriated to the bone by rough cord, and as it did not reach the ground, the portly bishop fell, and being much bruised, groaned piteously. Faithful friends and tried followers were waiting at the foot of the tower, where they had swift horses in readiness for him, though they were in great terror. Having mounted on horseback with them, they fled with the utmost speed, and escorted by his trusty companions, who had charge of his treasure, he lost no time in hastening on shipboard, and, crossing over to Normandy, presented himself to Duke Robert.

Source: Ordericus Vitalis. *The Ecclesiastical History of England and Normandy*. Bk. X, Ch. XVIII, pp. 279–81.

DOCUMENT 42
The Virtues of Good Grooming—an Escape

. . . the duke's [Duke William] enemies plotted his death, and their plan to force an entrance into his fortress in the night time; having first stationed four troops of soldiers outside to prevent his having any opportunity of avoiding his fate by flight. Meanwhile, the duke, in entire ignorance of the fatal trap contrived for him, paid a visit to a young girl to whom he was attached. The girl knew of the enemy's plot, and, as according to her custom she was bathing his head, shed tears. The young prince inquired of his mistress what caused her to weep, and between entreaties and threats, drew from her with great address all the particulars which she had learnt from his enemies relating to the plot against his life. Thereupon he seized his arms, without waiting to have his hair combed, and took the girl with him, lest she should incur any risk; and sent her under the care of a certain abbot to William, duke of Poitiers, a companion of his in the wars, of his own age, requesting him to procure for his liberator an honourable marriage, as if she were his own sister. And this was done.

Source: Ordericus Vitalis. *The Ecclesiastical History of England and Normandy*. Bk. XII, Ch. XLV, pp. 91–92.

DOCUMENT 43

The Tables Are Turned; an Inept Castellan and a Clever Governor, the Scots Take a Castle, and Are Trapped

Meanwhile a valiant squire of Scotland, by name Alexander Ramsay, set out with forty men, determined upon performing some gallant enterprise; he and all his party were well-mounted, and, after riding the whole night through bye roads, came to Berwick at daybreak, where they concealed themselves, and sent a spy to observe the state of the castle, who soon returned, reporting that there was no water in the ditches, and no one about. Upon hearing this, Ramsay and his companions left their place of concealment, and advancing, placed their ladders against the wall of the castle, which they entered, sword in hand, and then immediately hastened to the great tower, where Sir Robert Boynton, the governor slept. Sir Robert, hearing this door being cut down, and fancying that some of his own men wanted to murder him (for at the time he was very unpopular), leaped out a window into the castle ditch, and thus broke his neck. The guard of the castle became alarmed at the noise, sounded their trumpets, and cried out "Treason! Treason!"

John Bisset, the governor of the town of Berwick, heard the cry, and apprehending the cause of it, immediately armed himself; and having given orders for the supports of the bridge, which connected the castle with the town, to be broken down, sent off a messenger to Lord Percy at Alnwick, to request his immediate assistance. "Tell my Lord Percy," he said to the messenger, "the state you have left me in, and how the Scots are shut up in the castle, and cannot get away unless they leap the walls." Had not John Bisset acted so wisely, Alexander Ramsay and his men would have gained the whole town; but when they attempted to leave the castle, and for this purpose let down the bridge, the chains which supported it broke, for the pillars on which it should have rested were gone. Ramsay finding himself thus caught, determined to defend the castle, thinking that it would be strong enough to hold out until succour should come from Scotland.

Source: Jean Froissart. *The Chronicles of England, France, and Spain.* Pp. 150–51.

WOMEN IN POLITICS AND WAR

DOCUMENT 44
Matilda Governs Normandy while William Conquers England

Leaving the government of Normandy to his Queen Matilda, and his young son Robert, with a counsel of religious prelates and valiant nobles to be guardians of the state.

Source: Ordericus Vitalis. *The Ecclesiastical History of England and Normandy.* Bk. IV, Ch. IV, pp. 13–14.

DOCUMENT 45
A Militant Countess

1074

And earl Ralph [a conspirator against King William] also being in his earldom [of Norfolk] would have marched forth with his people; but the garrisons of the castles of England, and the inhabitants of the country came against him, and prevented his effecting anything, on which he took a ship at Norwich: and his wife remained in the castle, and held it till she obtained terms, and then she departed from England with all her adherents.

Source: *The Anglo-Saxon Chronicle.* P. 454.

DOCUMENT 46
Princess Sibylla Defends Tarragona

Meanwhile, during his [Robert Bordet, Prince of Tarragona] journey to Rome and return through Normandy [in 1128], where he went to muster his adherents, Tarragona was left to the custody of his wife Sibylla, daughter of William la Chèvre, who was not less distinguished for courage than for beauty. For while her husband was away, her watchfulness was unceasing; every night she put on a coat of mail of a man-at-arms, and taking a staff in her hand, mounted to the battlements, and going the rounds of the city walls, kept the sentries on alert, giving them strict charge, and cautioning them to be on the look out against any stratagems of the enemy. Praiseworthy conduct in so young a lady, thus to do her husband's behests with true faith and constant love, while she piously governed the people of God with everwatchful care!

Source: Ordericus Vitalis. *The Ecclesiastical History of England and Normandy.* Bk. XII.L, Ch. VI, pp. 117–18.

DOCUMENT 47
The Changing Fortunes of Civil War, and the Daring Escape of Empress Matilda from Oxford in 1140

1140

Now was England much divided, some held with the king and some with the empress, for when the king was in prison the earls and the great men thought that he would never more come out, and they treated with the empress, and brought her to Oxford, and gave her the town. When the king was out of prison he heard this, and he took his army and besieged her in the tower, and they let her down from the tower by night with ropes, and she stole away, and she fled: and she went on foot to Wallingford.

Source: *The Anglo-Saxon Chronicle.* Pp. 505–6.

DOCUMENT 48
The Heroic Countess of Montfort Saves Her Castle and Fights for Brittany

You have heard of the successful attempt which Lord Charles de Blois, with other lords of France, made upon the duchy of Brittany—how the men of Nantes betrayed the Earl of Montfort into their hands, and Lord Charles became possessed of that city. But though the Earl of Montfort was a prisoner, the countess was at large, and being most valiant woman, she resolved to resist the interest of France in Brittany. Accordingly, she sent Sir Amauri de Clisson to King Edward in England to entreat his assistance, upon condition that her young son should take for his wife one of the king's daughters, and give her the title Duchess of Brittany. When Sir Amauri de Clisson arrived Edward was in London feasting the Earl of Salisbury, who had just returned from prison; however, he lost no time in giving him an audience, and then ordered Sir Walter Manny to collect an army, and make every possible haste to carry assistance to the countess, who was at Hennebon, besieged by the forces of Lord Charles de Blois. For several days Lord Charles and his men had been encamped before the place, and were unable to make any effect upon it; the barriers resisted their utmost efforts. On every attack the countess, who had clothed herself in armour, and was mounted on a war-horse, galloped up and down the streets entreating and encouraging inhabitants to make a brave resistance; at her orders the ladies and other women carried paving stones of the streets to the ramparts, and threw them on the enemy. She also had pots of quick-lime brought to her for this purpose.

During the siege the countess performed a very gallant action; she had ascended a high tower to see how her people behaved, and having observed that all the lords and others of the enemy had quitted their tents, and were come to the assault, she immediately descended, mounted her horse, and having collected 300 horsemen about her, sailed out of Hennebon by a gate that was not attacked, and, galloping up to the tents, cut them down and set them on fire, without any loss to her own party. As soon as the French saw their camp in fire they left off assaulting the town, and hastened thither; but the countess and her little company made good their escape to Brest. Here she got together five or six hundred men, all well armed and mounted, and leaving Brest at midnight, went straight to Hennebon, which she reached about sunrise; the gates of the castle opened to receive her, and she entered in triumph amidst sounds of trumpets and other warlike instruments, to the great astonishment of the French, who knew nothing of her arrival, and who began arming themselves for another attack upon the town. This attack was very severe, and lasted till past noon. The French lost more than their opponents, and the Lord Charles, finding that much time was wasted, determined to leave Lord Lewis of Spain before Hennebon, whilst he went to besiege the castle of Aurai and other places. Lord Lewis kept up the siege vigorously, and made such progress by battering the walls with his engines, that the courage of those within began to falter; and all, with the exception of the countess, were wishing to surrender. Indeed, negotiations to that effect were actually going on, when the countess, looking out of a window towards the sea, exclaimed with joy, "I see the succour which I have so long expected." The town's-people ran to the ramparts, and saw a numerous fleet of great and small vessels, well-trimmed, making all the sail they could towards Hennebon, which they imagined must be a fleet from England; so long detained by tempests and contrary winds; and they were right in their conjectures, for in a few hours the English came on shore. No sooner had they landed than Sir Walter began in right earnest to assist the countess against the French. He inquired of her the state of the town, and of the enemy's army, and while engaged in conversation he chanced to look out the window, and seeing a large machine belonging to the enemy near the wall, vowed he would destroy it at once if any would second him. Two valiant knights were ready in the moment, and having armed themselves, they sallied quietly out of the city gates, taking with them 300 archers. These shot so true and well, that the machine was soon cleared of its defenders; the greater part of them were slain, and the large machine itself forthwith cut down and pulled to pieces. The gallant band then dashing in among the tents and huts, set fire to them, and killed and wounded many before the enemy was in motion. After this they made their retreat, but the French followed like madmen. Sir Walter seeing them, exclaimed, "May I never be embraced by my mistress if I enter the castle or fortress before I have unhorsed one of those gallopers," and so saying he turned, as did his companions—they spitted several coursers, and unhorsed many; after which they made good their escape to the castle, where the countess received them with a most cheerful countenance, and kissed Sir Walter and all his party, one after another, like a noble and valiant dame.

Source: Jean Froissart. *The Chronicles of England, France, and Spain.* Bk. II, pp. 34–36.

DOCUMENT 49
Countess Alberede Builds a Fine Castle and Then Has Her Architect Lanfred Beheaded so that He Cannot Build Another

This is the famous castle [of Ivri], of great size and strongly fortified, which was built by Alberede wife of Ralph, count of Bayeux, and of which Hugh, bishop of Bayeux [her son], and brother of John, archbishop of Rouen held for a long time against all the efforts of the dukes of Normandy. It is said that Alberede, having completed the fortress with vast labor and expense, caused Lanfred, whose character as an architect transcended that of all the other French architects at the time, and who after building the castle of Pithiviers was appointed master of these works, to be beheaded, that he might not erect a similar fortress anywhere else. She also, in the end, was put to death by her husband on account of the same castle of Ivri, having attempted to expel him from it.

Source: Ordericus Vitalis. *The Ecclesiastical History of England and Normandy.* Bk. VIII, Ch. XXIV, p. 25.

DOCUMENT 50
Isabel, a Warrior Countess, and Her Rival Stir up a Civil War

For there a worse than civil war was raged between two powerful brothers, and the mischief was fomented by the spiteful jealousy of their haughty wives. The Countess Havise took offense at some taunts uttered by Isabel de Conches, and used all of her influence with Count William and his barons to induce them to have recourse to arms. Thus, through women's slights and quarrels the hearts of brave men were stirred to rage, and their hands speedily imbrued in the blood of their fellow mortals, while burning farms and villages completed the horrors. Both the ladies who stirred up these fierce hostilities were great talkers, and spirited as well as handsome; they ruled their husbands, oppressed their vassals, and inspired terror in various ways. But still their characters were very different; Havise had wit and eloquence, but she was cruel and avaricious. On the contrary Isabel was generous, enterprising and gay, so that she was beloved and esteemed by those about her. She rode in knightly armour when the vassals took the field, and exhibited as much daring among belted knights and men-at-arms as Camilla, the renowned virgin of Italy among the squadrons of Turnus.

Source: Ordericus Vitalis. *The Ecclesiastical History of England and Normandy.* Bk. VIII, Ch. XIV, p. 494.

DOCUMENT 51
A Clever Mother, but Was She Wicked Too?

His wife Agnes was sister of Anselm de Ribemont, and fifteen years after their marriage gave birth to a son, who was named Walter. After his father's death, she carefully educated him until he arrived at manhood, and managed his hereditary domains for many years with great prudence. This lady, giving way to the feelings of her sex, formed an affection for Duke Robert, and entangled him in an illicit connection, by the blandishments of love. Promising him succour against his enemies, both from her own resources and those of her powerful relations, she induced the silly duke to engage that on the death of his present wife, he would not only marry her, but entrust to her the government of the whole of Normandy.

Not long afterwards the duchess Sibylla took to her bed, infected by poison, and died in the season of Lent, to the general sorrow.

Source: Ordericus Vitalis. *The Ecclesiastical History of England and Normandy.* Bk. XI, Ch. IV, p. 343.

DOCUMENT 52
Juliana, King Henry's Illegitimate Daughter, Tries to Shoot Her Father and Escapes by Way of the Moat

Juliana was now involved with anxieties, not knowing where to turn, and feeling sure that her father was deeply exasperated against her, and would never retire from the castle he had invested, but as a victor. At length, as Solomon says, "There is no wickedness like that of a woman," she determined on lifting her hands against the Lord's anointed. In consequence, she treacherously sought a conference with her father, and the king, who suspected no such fraudulent design in a woman, giving her the meeting, his unhappy daughter attempted his life. Drawing a cross-bow she launched a bolt at him, but through God's protection he escaped unharmed. Thereupon the king ordered the drawbridge of the castle to be broken down, so that no one could either enter or come out.

Juliana now finding herself blockaded on all points and that there was no one to succour her, surrendered the castle [of Breteuil] to the king; but he would on no account consent to allow her to depart freely: so that the king's orders compelled her to let herself down from the summit of the walls without support, and as there was no bridge she descended into the foss indecently, with naked legs. This took place in the beginning of Lent, the third week of February, when the castle-ditch was now full of snow-water which, being half frozen, her tender limbs of course suffered in her fall from the severity of the cold. The unfortunate heroine, getting out of it how she could and covered with shame, joined her husband who was than at Paci, and gave him a faithful account of the sad occurrence. Meanwhile, the king assembled the burgesses, commended them for maintaining their allegiance, honoured them with promises and benefits, and by their advice placed the castle of Breteuil in the custody of William, son of Ralph.

Source: Ordericus Vitalis. *The Ecclesiastical History of England and Normandy*. Bk. XII, Ch. X, pp. 466–67.

DOCUMENT 53
The Earl of Chester and His Brother Capture Lincoln Castle with the Help of Their Wives

In the year of our Lord 1141 . . . Ranulf, earl of Chester, and his half-brother William de Roumare, revolted against King Stephen, and surprised the fortress which he had at Lincoln for the defence of the city. Cautiously choosing a time when the garrison of the tower were dispersed abroad and engaged in sports, they sent their wives before them to the castle, under pretence of their taking amusement. While, however, the two countesses stayed there talking and joking with the wife of the knight whose duty it was to defend the tower, the earl of Chester came in, without his armour or even his mantle, apparently to fetch back his wife, attended by three soldiers, no one expecting any fraud. Having thus gained an entrance, they quickly laid hold of the bars and such weapons as were at hand, and forcibly ejected the king's guard. They then let in Earl William and his men-at-arms, as it had been planned before, and in this way the two brothers got possession of the tower and the whole city.

Source: Ordericus Vitalis. *The Ecclesiastical History of England and Normandy*. Bk. XIII, Ch. XLIII, pp. 214–16.

OTHER FORTIFIED PLACES

DOCUMENT 54
The Earl of Pembroke and His Men Find Shelter in a Fortified House

The earl [of Pembroke] and few knights were fortunate enough to escape, and sheltered themselves in an old house which belonged to the knights templars. The house was embattled, without a moat, and only enclosed with a stone wall; nevertheless they set up a brave defence.

The French tried by scaling ladders, and every means they could devise, to gain an entrance, but without effect; night overtook them, and they desisted, saying they had done enough for one day, and would return to attack to-morrow.

As soon as it was dark the Earl of Pembroke sent off one of his party to inform Sir John Chandos of the danger they were in, and beg his immediate assistance. The messenger took, as he thought, the direct road for Poitiers; but it so fell out that he wandered about the whole night until it was broad day, before he hit upon the right course. At sunrise the French prepared to renew the attack; however, the earl and his brave companions, instead of sleeping, had employed their time in fortifying the place with whatever they could lay hands upon, so that they were in a state to resist, which they did most manfully and to the great indignation of the besiegers. It was now evening, and the French finding the place still hold out, sent orders to all the villagers round about to bring pickaxes and mattocks, in order to undermine the walls. The English were more afraid of this than anything, and the earl determined to dispatch another messenger to Sir John; and addressing the squire who had undertaken the commission, he said, "Tell Sir John our condition, and recommend me to him by this token." He then took off his finger a rich gold ring, adding, "Give him this from me, he will know it well again." [The English are finally rescued.]

Source: Jean Froissart. *The Chronicles of England, France, and Spain*. Pp. 123–24.

DOCUMENT 55
City Walls

I [Anna] must describe in a few words the appearance of the city of Dyrrachium. The walls were flanked by towers standing up above it all around and rising as high as eleven feet, which were ascended by a spiral stair and strengthened by battlements. Such was the appearance and defence of the city. The thickness of the walls was remarkable, in fact so great was its width that more than four horseman could ride abreast on it quite safely.

Source: Anna Comnena. *The Alexiad*. Bk. XIII, p. 330.

DOCUMENT 56
The Destruction of Limerick

[Raymond] voluntarily gave it [the city of Limerick] in charge to Duvenald prince of Thomond, as baron of the lord and king of England, on his taking a solemn oath to preserve the place in good condition, restore it to the king when required, and keep the peace, for which he gave fresh hostages, and renewed in various forms the solemn oaths he had before sworn.

Scarcely, however, had the garrison been withdrawn and passed the further end of the bridge, when it was broken down behind them, and they beheld with grief that noble city, so well fortified, containing such fair buildings, and stored with all manner of provisions collected from all quarters, given to the flames, fire being set to it in four places. It was the work of the traitorous Duvenald, who thus openly showed by his new and disgraceful perfidy, what little reliance could be placed on the Irish faith.

Source: Giraldus Cambrensis. *The Conquest of Ireland.* Ch. XIV, pp. 272–73.

LIFE IN THE TOWN AND COUNTRYSIDE

DOCUMENT 57
The Building of a Town

The market, also, which in the days of his [Baldwin II, Count of Guines] predecessors had been at Sutquerque not for any special cause but because of chance, he changed to Andruicq, but following the advice of the church did not change the day [of the market]. There assembled and came to reside those living round about as citizens. Also the Count of Guines as much for heavenly glory as for a virtuous deed ordered a public fair to be held each year in that place during the feast of the solemnity of the Pentecost for all the people, as much merchants as others, for the abundance of merchandise which came from all parts, and to this decree he confirmed by oath. The town he surrounded by a double ditch and rampart, in the midst of which he built homes and necessary buildings and he built with diligent and reverent care a chapel at the entrance of the first enclosure, as was fitting, to the honor of the holy Nicollas; there he placed a holy man named Estienne as chaplain, with sufficient books and various ecclesiastical ornaments, to the eternal glory of the holy city above. So he found a means by thought and force to drain off a marsh with Herculean efforts and make it fertile.

Source: Lambert, cure of Ardre. *The Chronicle of Guines and of Ardre.* Ch. LXXVIII, p. 55.

DOCUMENT 58
The Origin of Oven Dues—the Bear and the Bread

[Arnold went to England where the king made him a present of a huge bear]. [The bear], when he was being shown and led before the people, amused the crowd much and pleased them . . . they were not able to [see him] on account of those who guarded him for the lord, if he did not receive a loaf for feeding the beast from each one who saw the spectacle; . . . so the foolish people, churchmen as well as nobles, voluntarily promised the lord of Ardre to give to the guards of the bear for each batch of bread to be baked in the town oven a loaf of bread for the support of the bear so that they might be entertained by its appearance on feast days and take pleasure to see it fight. . . . [Even after the bear died, the people had to pay a bread tax.] Without pleasure which the miserable bear might give the people the bread for the bear is claimed by the lord, and customarily collected by the law . . . as a relic of ancient dues and customs.

Source: Lambert, cure of Ardre. *The Chronicle of Guines and of Ardre.* Ch. CXXVIII, pp. 103–4.

DOCUMENT 59
A City Is Forced to Feed the Army

. . . It was determined to open a treaty with the inhabitants of Rheims [Reims, France], in order to induce them to supply the army with provisions; but they refused to enter into any negotiation, and in reply said that the English must make the best of their own case. This answer was so galling, that in one week the English light troops burnt upwards of sixty villages dependent upon Rheims; moreover, having heard that 6,000 sheep had been secured in the ditches of that town, the vanguard advanced thither and drove them off, without anyone daring to come out from the town to prevent them; for the archers who were posted on the banks of the ditch shot so sharply that the bulwarks were quite cleared. Having gained this success, the English sent to inform the townsmen that they would burn all the standing corn [grain] unless they ransomed it by sending bread and wine. At this they were so much alarmed, that they immediately sent off from ten to sixteen carts of provisions.

Source: Jean Froissart. *The Chronicles of England, France, and Spain.* P. 178.

DOCUMENT 60
A Rare Description of a Poor Woman's House; the Earl Takes Refuge

The earl [of Flanders] himself went up a by-street, where he changed dresses with one of his servants, commanding the fellow at the same time to be silent on the subject should he chance to fall into the hands of the enemy. All this while the men of Ghent were going up and down the streets searching everywhere they could think of in order to find the earl; indeed, he was in the greatest danger, and it was God alone who watched over him and delivered him from his perilous situation. After rambling some time through the streets, and hiding himself in different corners not knowing what course to take, he entered the house of a poor woman— a very unfit habitation for so mighty a lord, for it contained but one room, over which was a sort of garret to be approached only by means of a lad-der of seven steps, where, on a miserable bed, the children of this poor woman lay. It was with fear and trembling that the earl entered the hovel; and making his case known to the woman said, "Good woman, save me: I am thy lord, the Earl of Flanders, but at this moment in the greatest distress. I must hide myself, for my enemies are in pursuit of me, and I will handsomely reward you for any favor you may grant." The poor woman knew the earl well for she had frequently received alms at his door, and also seen him pass and repass when going out hunting. Moved at his condition, therefore, she admitted him most willingly. And as it turned out, it was very fortunate for him that she did so, for had she de-layed her answer but one moment, the enemies would have found him in conversation with her. "My lord," she said, "mount this ladder, and get under the bed in which my children sleep." This the earl did, while the poor woman employed herself by the fire-side with another child in a cra-dle; and scarcely had the earl concealed himself, when the mob entered the house; for one of them had seen a man go in there.

Source: Jean Froissart. *The Chronicles of England, France, and Spain.* P. 241.

DOCUMENT 61
Homes in the Countryside

[T]hey [the Welsh] neither inhabit towns, villages, nor castles, but lead a solitary life in the woods, on the borders of which they do not erect sumptuous palaces, nor lofty stone buildings, but content themselves with small huts made of the boughs of trees twisted together, constructed with little labour and expense, and sufficient to endure throughout the year. They have neither orchards nor gardens, but gladly eat the fruit of both when given to them. The greater part of their land is laid down to pasturage; little is cultivated, a very small quantity is ornamented with flowers, and a still smaller is sown.

Source: Giraldus Cambrensis. *Description of Wales*. Ch. XVII, pp. 505–6.

DOCUMENT 62
The Welsh Character, Hospitality, and Personal Hygiene

[Ch. IX] Not addicted to gluttony or drunkenness, this people, who incur no expense in food or dress, and whose minds are always bent upon the defence of their country, and on the means of plunder, are wholly employed in the care of their horses and furniture. . . .

[Ch. X] No one of this nation ever begs, for the houses of all are common to all; and they consider liberality and hospitality amongst the virtues.

. . . Those who arrive in the morning are entertained till evening with the conversation of young women, and the music of the harp; for each house has its young women and harps allotted for that purpose . . . in each family the art of playing on the harp is held preferable to any other learning.

. . . While the family is engaged in waiting on the guests, the host and hostess stand up, paying unremitting attention to every thing, and take no food till all the company are satisfied; that in case of deficiency, it may fall upon them. A bed made of rushes, and covered with a coarse kind of cloth manufactured in the country called brychan, is then placed along the side of the room, and they all in common lie down to sleep; nor is their dress at night different from that by day, for at all seasons they defend themselves from the cold by only a thin cloak or tunic. The fire continues to burn by night as well as by day, at their feet, and they receive much comfort from the natural heat of the persons lying near them. . . .

[Ch. XI] Both sexes exceed any other nation in attention to their teeth, which they render like ivory, by constantly rubbing them with green hazel and wiping with woolen cloth. For their better preservation they abstain from hot meats, and eat only such as are cold, warm, or temperate. The men shave all their beard except the moustaches.

Source: Giraldus Cambrensis. *Description of Wales*. Ch. IX, X, XI, pp. 492–94.

THE NOBLES, ENTERTAINMENT, AND BANQUETS

DOCUMENT 63
Noble Entertainments

Refreshed by their banqueting, they go forth into the fields without the city, and sundry among them fall to playing at sundry manner games. Presently the knights engage in a game on horseback, making show of fighting a battle whilst the dames and damsels looking on from the top of the walls, for whose sake the courtly knights make believe to be fighting, do cheer them on for the sake of seeing the better sport. Others elsewhere spend the rest of the day in shooting arrows, some in tilting spears, some in flinging heavy stones, some in putting the weight; others again in playing at the dice or in a diversity of other games, but all without wrangling; and whosoever had done best in his own game was presented by Arthur with a boon of price.

Source: Geoffrey of Monmouth. *History of the Kings of Britain*. Ch. XIV, p. 171.

DOCUMENT 64
A Poet Suffers for His Jokes

After Easter, the king [Henry] pronounced judgment at Rouen on the captive culprits, causing the eyes of Godfrey de Tourville and Odard du Pin to be put out for the treason of which they had been guilty. He also deprived of sight Luke de la Barre, for having ridiculed him in his songs, and engaged in rash enterprises against him.

[King Henry said,] "Luke, indeed never did me homage, but he was in arms against me at Pontaudemer; after which, when peace was concluded, I excused all forfeitures, and suffered them to go free, with their horses, arms and baggage. But Luke immediately rejoined my enemies, and, in conjunction with them, stirred up fresh hostilities against me, adding to his former offences such as were still worse. Besides, the merry glee-man made scurrilous sonnets on me, and sang them aloud to bring me into contempt, thus making me the laughing-stock of my malicious enemies. Now God has delivered him into my hands for chastisement."

. . . The unhappy Luke, when he found himself sentenced to lose his eyes, preferred death to life in perpetual darkness, and made all the resistance he could to the executioners when they attempted to mutilate him. At last, after struggling with them, he dashed his head against the stone walls, and, like one demented, fracturing his skull, thus miserably expired, lamented by many who admired his worth and playful wit.

Source: Ordericus Vitalis. *The Ecclesiastical History of England and Normandy.* Bk. XII, Ch. XXXXIX, pp. 75–76.

DOCUMENT 65
A Noble Household Finds Lodging, and the Dangers of Spanish Wine in the Fourteenth Century

It was told me that the duke, duchess, and the ladies Constance and Philippa, were lodged in the abbey, and held their court there. Sir John Holland and Sir Thomas Moreaux, with their ladies, lodged in the town; the other barons and knights as they could, and the men-at-arms quartered in the plain round the town; those who could not find houses built huts of the boughs of trees, and made themselves comfortable with what they could get. Meat and strong wines were in abundance; the archers drank so much that they were the greater part of their time in bed drunk; and very often from taking too much new wine, they had fevers, and in the morning such headaches, as to prevent them from doing anything the remainder of the day.

Source: Jean Froissart. *The Chronicles of England, France, and Spain*. Pp. 344–45.

DOCUMENT 66
A Description of a Livery

The different townsmen wore liveries and arms, to distinguish them from one another. Some had jackets of blue and yellow, others wore a welt of black on a red jacket, others chevroned with white on a blue coat, others green and blue, others lozenged with black and white, others quartered red and white, others all blue.

Source: Jean Froissart. *The Chronicles of England, France, and Spain*. P. 253.

DOCUMENT 67
The Lord at Dinner

When he [Count Gaston Phoebus de Foix] quitted his chamber at midnight for supper, twelve servants bore each lighted torch before him. The hall was full of knights and squires, and there were plenty of tables laid out for any of those who chose to sup. No one spoke to him at table unless he first began the conversation. He ate heartily of poultry, but only the wings and thighs. He had great pleasure in hearing minstrels, being himself a proficient in the science. He remained at table about two hours, and was pleased whenever fanciful dishes were served up to him—not that he desired to partake of them, but having seen them, he immediately sent them to the tables of his knights and squires. In short, everything considered, though I had been in several courts, I was never at one that pleased me more.

Source: Jean Froissart. *The Chronicles of England, France, and Spain*. P. 305.

DOCUMENT 68
A Great Banquet in Thirteenth-Century France, the Social and Architectural Arrangements

Now let us return to our subject and tell how, after these things, the king [Louis IX] held a full court at Saumur in Anjou, and I was there and can testify that it was the best-ordered court that ever I saw. For at the king's table ate, after him, the Count of Poitiers, whom he had newly made knight at the feast of St. John; and after the Count of Poitiers, ate the Count of Dreux, whom he had also newly made knight; and after the Count of Dreux the Count of la Marche; and after the Count of la Marche the good Count Peter of Brittany; and before the king's table, opposite the Count of Dreux, ate my lord the King of Naverre, in tunic and mantle of samite well bedight with a belt and a clasp, and a cap of gold; and I carved before him.

Before the king the Count of Artois, his brother, served the meat, and before the king the good count John of Soissons carved with a knife. In order to guard the king's table there were there my Lord Imbert of Beaujeu, who was afterwards Constable of France, and my Lord Enguerrand of Coucy, and my Lord Archamband of Bourbon. Behind these three barons stood some thirty of their knights, in tunics of silken cloth, to keep guard over them; and behind these knights there were a great quantity of sergeants bearing on their clothing the arms of the Count of Poitiers embroidered in taffeta. The king was clothed in a tunic of blue satin, and surcoat and mantle of vermeil samite lined with ermine, and he had a cotton cap on his head, which suited him very badly, because he was at that time a young man.

The king held these banquets in the halls of Saumur which had been built, so it was said, by the great King Henry of England [Henry II] in order that he might hold his great banquets therein; and this hall is built after the fashion of the cloisters of the white monks of the Cistercian order. But I think there is none other hall so large, and by a great deal. And I will tell you why I think so—it is because by the wall of the cloister, where the king ate, surrounded by his knights and sergeants who occupied a great space, there was also room for a table where ate twenty bishops and archbishops . . . the Queen Blanche, the king's mother, ate near their table, at the end of the cloister, on the other side from the king.

And to serve the queen there was the Count of Boulogne, who afterwards became King of Portugal, and the good Count Hugh of St. Paul, and a German of the age of eighteen years, who was said to be the son of St. Elizabeth of Thuringia, for which cause it was told that Queen Blanche kissed him on the forehead, as an act of devotion, because she thought that his mother must ofttimes have kissed him there.

At the end of the cloister, on the other side, were the kitchens, cellars, the pantries and the butteries; from this end were served to the king and to the queen meats, and wine, and bread. And in the wings and in the central court ate the knights, in such numbers, that I knew not how to count them. And many said they had never, at any feast, seen together so many surcoats and other garments, of cloth of gold and silk; and it was said also that no less than three thousand knights were there present.

Source: Jean de Joinville. *Chronicle of the Crusade of St. Louis*. Pp. 159–60.

DOCUMENT 69
A Splendid Royal Banquet and Entertainment, June 20, 1399

Shortly after mass the king, queen and all the ladies entered the hall: and you must know that the great marble table which is in the hall was covered with oaken planks four inches thick, and the royal dinner placed thereon. Near the table, and against one of the pillars, was the king's buffet, magnificently decked out with gold and silver plate; and in the hall were plenty of attendants, sergeants-at-arms, ushers, archers, and minstrels, who played away to the best of their ability. The kings, prelates, and ladies, having washed, seated themselves at the tables, which were three in number: at the first, sat the King and Queen of France, and some few of higher nobility; and at the other two, there were upwards of 500 ladies and damsels; but the crowd was so great that it was with difficulty they could be served with dinner, which indeed was plentiful and sumptuous. There were in the hall many curiously arranged devices: a castle to represent the city of Troy, with the palace of Ilion, from which were displayed the banners of the Trojans; also a pavilion on which were placed the banners of the Grecian kings, and which was moved as it were by invisible beings to the attack of Troy, assisted by a large ship capable of containing 100 men-at-arms; but the crowd was so great that this amusement could not last long. There were so many people on all sides that several were stifled by the heat, and the queen herself almost fainted. The queen left the palace about five o'clock, and, followed by her ladies, in litters or on horseback, proceeded to the residence of the king at the hotel de St. Pol. The king took boat at the palace, and was rowed to his hotel, where, in a large hall, he entertained the ladies at the banquet; the queen however, remained in her chamber where she supped, and did not again appear that night.

Source: Jean Froissart. *The Chronicles of England, France, and Spain.* Pp. 462–63.

DOCUMENT 70
The Dance of the Flaming Wildmen: A Wedding Party Ends in Tragedy, January 1392

. . . a marriage took place between a young squire of Vermandois and a damsel of the queen, both of the royal household; the court was much pleased at it, and the king [Charles VI] resolved that the wedding feast should be kept at his expense. It was held at the hotel of St. Pol, and great crowds of nobility attended, among whom were the Dukes of Orleans, Berry, and Burgundy, with their duchesses. The wedding-day was passed in dancing and rejoicing; the king entertained the queen at supper in great state, and everyone exerted himself to add to the gaiety, seeing how much delighted the king appeared. There was in the king's household a Norman squire [Hugonin de Guisay], a near relative of the bridegroom, who thought of the following piece of pleasantry to amuse the king and ladies. In the evening he provided six coats of linen covered in fine flax the colour of hair; in one of them he dressed the king, and the Count of Joigny, a young and gallant knight in another, Sir Charles of Poitiers had a third, Sir Yoain de Foix the fourth, the son of the Lord de Nantouillet, a young knight, had the fifth, and Hugonin dressed himself in the sixth. When thus dressed they appeared like savages, for they were covered with hair from head to foot. This masquerade pleased the king greatly, and he expressed his pleasure to his squire; it was so secretly contrived that no one knew anything of the matter but the servants who attended them. Word was sent to the room where the ladies were, commanding in the king's name that all the torches should be placed on one side, and that no person come near the six savage men who were about to enter; the torchbearers, therefore, withdrew on one side, and no one approached the dancers so long as the savages stayed in the room. The apartment was now clear of all but the ladies, damsels, and knights and squires, who were dancing with them. Soon after the Duke of Orleans entered, attended by four knights and six torches, ignorant of the orders that had been given, and of the entrance of the savages; he first looked at the dancing, and then took part himself, just as the King of France made his appearance with five others dressed like savages, and covered from head to foot with flax to represent hair; not one person in the company knew them, and they were all fastened together, while the king led them dancing. Everyone was so occupied in examining them, that the order about the torches was forgotten; the king, who was their leader, fortunately for him, advanced to show himself to the ladies, and passing by the queen, placed himself near the Duchess of Berry, who, though his aunt, was the youngest of the company. The duchess amused herself in talking with him, and as the king rose up, not wishing to discover himself, the duchess said, "You shall not escape thus; I will know your name."

At this moment a most unfortunate accident befell the others, through the youthful gaiety of the Duke of Orleans, who, could he have foreseen the mischief he was about to cause, would not on any consideration have acted so. Being very inquisitive to find out who they were, while the five were dancing he took one of the torches from his servants, and holding it too near, set their dresses on fire. Flax, you know, is instantly in a blaze, and the pitch with which the cloth had been covered to fasten the flax added to the impossibility of extinguishing it. They were likewise chained together, and their cries were dreadful; some knights did their utmost to disengage them, but the fire was so strong that they burnt their hands very severely. One of the five, Nantouillet, broke the chain, and rushing into the buttery, flung himself into a large tub of water, which was there for washing dishes and plates; this saved him, or he would have burnt to death like the rest, but he was, withal, very ill for some time. The queen was so much alarmed that she fainted, for she knew the king was one of the six; the Duchess of Berry, however, saved the king by throwing the train of her robe over him. This terrible accident happened about twelve o'clock at night, in the ball-room of the hotel de St. Pol, and it was a most melancholy spectacle—of the four that were on fire, two died on the spot; the other two, the bastard of Foix and the Count of Joigny, were carried to their hotels, and died two days afterwards in great agonies.

Source: Jean Froissart. *The Chronicles of England, France, and Spain.* Pp. 511–12.

GLOSSARY

Aisle: A passage or corridor.

Apse: A large niche; in a Christian church, the semicircular area around the altar.

Arrow slit: An opening in a wall through which an archer shoots, found in **merlons** and **wall passages**.

Ashlar masonry: Finely cut and finished blocks of stone, laid in even courses to produce a smooth wall.

Bailey: The area enclosed by the castle walls, the yard, also called a **ward** in England.

Ballista: A stone-throwing machine, working on the principle of a catapult or sling shot.

Barbican: The fortification in front of a gateway or the forward extension of a **gatehouse**.

Barmkyn (barmkin): The walled courtyard of a Scottish **tower house**.

Barrel vault: A tunnel-like masonry covering, shaped like a half cylinder.

Bastide: A new town established by the king and often fortified.

Bastion: A low broad earth and masonry tower; a platform to support cannon.

Battlements: Fortified wall tops, including the **wall-walk, crenellations,** and **machicolations** or **hoardings.**

Bay: In architecture, a unit of space defined by architectural elements.

Bay window: A window that projects out from the wall.

Belfrey: A movable wooden siege tower from which warriors can attack the walls and towers of a castle.

Brattice: A short section of **hoardings** or **machicolations,** usually over a door.

Buttery: The room for storing and assembling beverages (beer and ale). *See also* **pantry** and **kitchen.**

Buttress: An architectural support for masonry acting through shear weight and mass.

Casemate: The defenses and rooms built at the base of a wall.

Cat: A moveable fireproofed shed or roof used to protect men **sapping** or battering castle walls.

Chamber block: A separate residential building in the **bailey** containing the living rooms.

Clerestory: The window-wall above the aisle roofs.

Concentric castle: A castle having two rings of walls, one within the other.

Courtyard: The open space within the castle walls; the central open court in a building.

Crenel, crenellation: The notched wall in front of the **wall-walk**, consisting of **merlons** (the taller section) and crenels (the lower section).

Curtain wall: A castle wall between towers.

Dais: A raised platform at the end of the **hall**, supporting the high table, throne, or seat of judgment.

Demesne: The estate or property of the lord, worked by peasants.

Donjon: A French term for the largest and most important tower of a castle; the great tower.

Drawbridge: A bridge that can be lifted to prevent passage over a ditch or moat.

Embankment: An earthen wall or rampart, usually topped with walls or **palisades**.

Embrasure: A recess in a wall; an angled opening in the thickness of the wall for windows or **arrow slits**. Window seats turn the space into a small, private room.

Enceinte: The defensive enclosure; a castle consisting of a towered wall without a **great tower**.

Fighting gallery: The passage at the top of walls with wooden **hoardings** or stone **machicolations**.

Forebuilding: A castle-like building in front of, and protecting, the entrance to the main castle.

Fort, fortress: A military establishment housing a garrison, in contrast to a castle which is private and staffed by a castle guard.

Gallery: A passage open on one side; often with an arcade; a long room; a loggia.

Garderobe: A toilet or latrine.

Gatehouse: A fortified entrance building, sometimes including the commander's residence.

Glacis: The sloping lower wall, also called a **talus**.

Gloriette: A small residence or party house built on an island.

Great tower: The principal building in a castle; the castle's strong point and place of last retreat; later, the largest and most important tower; later called a keep or a donjon.

Groin vault: A vault, constructed by crossing two barrel vaults of equal size; permits windows.

Hall: The principal building or room in a castle, combining domestic, administrative, judicial, and festive functions.

Heraldry: A system of symbolic identification.

Hoarding: A temporary timber gallery built at the top of a wall to provide extra space for archers and other warriors when the castle is attacked.

Invest: To lay siege to a castle by cutting off all means of supply and reinforcement.

Justiciar: A governor or viceroy.

Keep: An English term for the most important tower of a castle. The **great tower**.

Killing ground: Territory beyond a castle wall within the range of archers or gunners.

Kitchen: Room where food is prepared. Because of the danger of fire, kitchens and ovens were usually separate buildings; when attached, the kitchen was separated from the hall by the **screens passage**.

License to crenellate: The official permission to fortify an existing structure or to build a fortified dwelling.

Lime wash: A waterproof, whitewash wall covering.

List: The space between two walls; **Lists:** a place for jousting surrounded by walls. *See also* **tiltyard.**

Livery: The distinctive dress identifying the followers of a lord.

Loggia: An open gallery; a porch.

Loophole: An **arrow slit** enlarged for use by crossbowmen or gunners.

Machicolation: Hoardings converted to stone to form a **fighting gallery** projecting from the top of the wall; part of the **battlements.**

Mangonel: A stone-throwing machine, working on the principle of torsion.

Manor house: The residence of the owner of an agricultural estate.

Masonry: Building with stone, brick and mortar, or concrete.

Merlon: The raised (taller) section of a crenellated wall. *See also* **crenel.**

Minstrels' gallery: The platform for musicians, often over the **screens passage.**

Moat: The ditch formed when mounds or embankments are raised; may be dry or filled with water.

Motte: The mound or artificial earthen hill on which a tower is built.

Motte-and-bailey castle: A castle consisting of a **great tower** on a **motte** with a walled space (**bailey**) beside or around it.

Mural towers: Towers attached to and forming part of a wall.

Murder holes: Holes in the vault built over a passageway through which missiles could be dropped or water poured to douse fires.

Nave: The central aisle of a building; rises above the side aisles.

Newel stairs: A spiral staircase. *See also* **stairs.**

Oriel window: A window that projects from the wall in an upper story, either cantilevered out or supported on a bracket (in contrast to a bay window, which extends to the ground).

Pale: The boundary line or wall marking the territory of town.

Palisade (Latin: *palus*-stake): A wall of upright stakes, a stockade.

Pantry: A room for storing and preparing bread and other foods. *See also* **buttery** and **screens passage.**

Parapet: A defensive wall built on the outer side of the **wall-walk** along the top of a wall.

Penthouse, pentise, pentice: A moveable wooden shed with a sloping roof. *See also* **cat** and **turtle.**

Petraria: The general term for stone-throwing machines.

Pier: A masonry support made up of stones or rubble and concrete, in contrast to a column which is formed by a single stone or stacked drums of stone.

Pilaster: A masonry half column or rectangular panel attached to a wall for its decorative effect.

Pipe rolls: Royal accounts.

Portcullis: A sliding timber and metal grille in front of and protecting a castle door.

Postern: A hidden back door, a **sally port**.

Presence chamber: A room where the king or lord met distinguished visitors and conducted business, usually preceded by a waiting room.

Privy chamber: A private room; a "privy" can be a synonym for **garderobe**.

Putlog, putlog hole: A putlog is a beam that supports scaffolding or hoardings; the beam is inserted into a permanent hole in the masonry wall.

Ribbed vault: A vault supported and reinforced by additional masonry arches.

Sally port: A small hidden door in the castle wall used by defenders making a "sally" or surprise attack; a **postern**.

Sap, sapper: To dig a tunnel; a sapper is the person who digs the tunnel.

Scaling ladder: A ladder used to climb castle walls.

Screens, screens passage: A wooden or masonry wall separating the hall from the service rooms; the passage created by the wall, leading to the **pantry, buttery,** and **kitchens**. A **minstrels' gallery** may be built above it.

Scriptorium: A room used for writing.

Shell keep: A stone enclosure without a **great tower**; usually on a mound; additional buildings may be built against the inside of the wall.

Shooting gallery: A corridor at the top of the castle wall, used by archers.

Siege: The blockade of a castle or town.

Siege castle, siege fort: A temporary fort; built by the besieging army to protect its camp; also a platform for siege engines.

Siege engines: Devices and machines created for use in siege warfare to attack walls and towns. *See also* **ballista, belfrey, mangonel, petraria, trebuchet.**

Slight, slighting: Official destruction of a castle.

Stairs, stair turret: Straight stairs were built within walls; spiral or **newel stairs** were built in a tower or turret; spiral stairs usually rose in a clockwise spiral so that a defender facing downward had space for his sword arm.

Talus: An outward sloping wall. *See also* **glacis.**

Tiltyard: A walled space for jousting. *See also* **list.**

Tournament: Jousting competition; originally training for warfare, later a popular medieval sporting event.

Tower house: A residential tower, with stacked **hall,** chambers, and service rooms.

Trebuchet: A stone-throwing machine working on the principle of counterweight.

Turret: A small tower attached to a wall or another tower.

Turtle: A moveable protective roof for **siege engines.**

Vault: The arched masonry covering over an interior space. *See also* **barrel vault, groin vault, ribbed vault.**

Voussoirs: Wedge-shaped blocks forming an arch. The center voussoir is called the keystone.

Wall passage: A corridor within the thickness of the wall.

Wall-walk: A walkway along the top of a wall, protected by the **parapet;** part of the **battlements.**

Ward: The **bailey**; the area within the castle walls.

Water gate: A fortified gate leading to quays on a river or seaside, for use of people and supplies arriving by boat.

Wicket: A small door within another door; a small gate in a fence.

Yett: The grille protecting a door in a Scottish **tower house**.

ANNOTATED BIBLIOGRAPHY

Reference

The Dictionary of Art. 34 vols. New York: Grove Dictionaries, 1996. Articles on all aspects of art and architecture.

Encyclopedia of World Art. 16 vols. New York: McGraw Hill, 1972–83. Articles on all aspects of art and architecture.

Fossier, Robert, ed. *The Cambridge Illustrated History of the Middle Ages*. 3 vols. Translated by Janet Sondheimer and Sarah Hanbury Tension. Cambridge, UK: Cambridge University Press, 1986–97. An authoritative historical survey.

Friar, Stephen. *The Sutton Companion to Castles*. Phoenix Mill, UK: Sutton Publishing, 2003. Over 1,000 entries including castles of England and Wales. Definitions and essays on individual topics arranged alphabetically. Friar provides wide-ranging essays on every aspect of castles, their uses and construction and design.

Holmes, G., ed. *The Oxford Illustrated History of Medieval Europe*. Oxford: Oxford University Press, 1988. An authoritative and interesting survey.

Hooper, N., and M. Bennett. *Warfare in the Middle Ages, 768–1487*, Cambridge Illustrated Atlas. Cambridge, UK: Cambridge University Press, 1996. A useful illustrated survey.

Kibler, William, and Grover A. Zinn. *Medieval France, an Encyclopedia*. New York and London: Garland, 1995. Articles on aspects of culture, art, and architecture.

Stenton, (Sir) Frank. *The First Century of English Feudalism, 1066–1300*. 2nd ed. Oxford: Clarendon Press, 1961. A classic, a little dated, but useful.

Primary Documents: Histories

The Anglo-Saxon Chronicle. Translated by Rev. James Ingram. London: J. M. Dent; New York: E. P. Dutton, 1913.

Anna Comnena. *The Alexiad of the Princess Anna Comnena.* Translated by Elizabeth A. S. Dawes. London: Kegan Paul, Trench, Trubner, 1928.

Bede. *Bede's Ecclesiastical History of England.* Translated by J. A. Giles. London: George Bell, 1903.

Froissart, Jean. *The Chronicles of England, France, and Spain by Sir John Froissart.* Translated by Thomas Johnes. New York: The Colonial Press, c. 1901; London: J. M. Dent; New York: E. P. Dutton, 1906.

Geoffrey of Monmouth. *History of the Kings of Britain by Geoffrey of Monmouth.* Translated by Sebastian Evans. London: J. M. Dent; New York: E. P. Dutton, 1911.

Giraldus Cambrensis (Gerald of Wales). *The Historical Works of Giraldus Cambrensis. Containing the Topography of Ireland, and the History of the Conquest of Ireland, translated by Thomas Forester. The Itinerary through Wales, and The Description of Wales, translated by Richard Colt Hoare.* Revised and edited by Thomas Wright. London: H. G. Bohn, 1863.

Joinville, Jean. *Chronicles of the Crusades by Villehardouin and De Joinville.* Translated by Sir Frank Marzials. London: J. M. Dent; New York: E. P. Dutton, 1908.

Lambert, cure of Ardre. *The Chronicle of Guines and of Ardre.* Translated by Majel Irene Kurrie. Master's thesis, University of Chicago, 1925.

Ordericus Vitalis. *The Ecclesiastical History of England and Normandy by Ordericus Vitalis.* Translated by Thomas Forester. London: Henry G. Bohn, 1856.

Literary Descriptions

Chretien de Troyes. *Perceval.* Translated by Burton Raffel. New Haven: Yale University Press, 1999.

———. *Yvain, the Knight of the Lion.* Translated by Burton Raffel. New Haven: Yale University Press, 1987.

Lorris, Guillaume de, and Jean de Meun. *The Romance of the Rose.* Translated by Harry W. Robbins, edited with an introduction by Charles W. Dunn. New York: E. P. Dutton, 1962. A description of noble gardens and the castle of Jealousy.

Malory, Sir Thomas. *The Works*. Edited by Eugene Vinaver, rev. P.C.C. Freld. 3 vols. Oxford: Clarendon Press, 1990. Stories of King Arthur and his knights.

Martorell, Joanot. *Tirant Lo Blanc*. Translated by David H. Rosenthal. Baltimore: Johns Hopkins University Press, 1996. Highly romanticized chivalric adventures.

The Poem of the Cid. Translated by Lesley Byrd Simpson. Berkeley and Los Angeles: University of California Press, 1957. The life and battles of a great warrior, his wife, and his daughters.

Sir Gawain and the Green Knight. Translated with an introduction by Burton Raffel Brian Storey. New York: Penguin Classics.

Tennyson, Alfred Lord. *Idylls of the King*. Edited by J. M. Gray. New Haven: Yale University Press, 1983. The Victorian version of King Arthur and the Knights of the Round Table.

Medieval Art and Architecture: General Studies

Alexander, Johnathan, and Paul Binski, eds. *Age of Chivalry, Art in Plantagenet England, 1200–1400*. London: Royal Academy of Arts, 1987. The second of three exhibitions covering the years 1066–1547. Interpretive essays over the period 1200–1400. See also Marks and Zarnecki.

Andrews, Francis B. *The Medieval Builder and His Methods*. New York: 1993. Practical information and technical descriptions of building techniques.

Calkins, Robert. *Medieval Architecture in Western Europe: From A.D. 300 to 1500*. New York: Oxford University Press, 1998. A survey of medieval architecture. Most of the photographs are taken by the author for this book.

Clifton-Taylor, Alec. *The Pattern of English Building*. London: Faber and Faber, 1972. Technical details and descriptions of the materials used by the builders.

Coldstream, Nicola. *Masons and Sculptors*, Medieval Craftsmen. London: British Museum Press, 1991. Part of the popular British Museum Series, well illustrated and authoritative.

———. *Medieval Architecture*, Oxford History of Art. Oxford: Oxford University Press, 2002. A sophisticated study including architectural symbolism and a study of the palace in Paris.

Harvey, John. *Mediaeval Gardens*. London: B. T. Batsford, 1981. Includes palace gardens.

Mancoff, Debra. *The Arthurian Revival in Victorian Art*. New York: Garland Publishing, 1990. The social background of the medieval revival in England. The focus is on painting. Includes an account of the Eglinton Tournament.

Marks, Richard, and Paul Williamson, eds. Assisted by Eleanor Townsend. *Gothic Art for England 1400–1547*. London: V & A Publications, 2003. The third of three exhibitions covering the years 1066–1547. Interpretive essays cover the period 1400–1554. See also Alexander and Zarnecki.

McLean, Teresa. *Medieval English Gardens*. New York: Viking Press, 1980. Includes palace gardens.

Stalley, Roger. *Early Medieval Architecture*, Oxford History of Art. Oxford: Oxford University Press, 1999. The finest study of early medieval architecture in print today. Includes castles.

Stokstad, Marilyn. *Medieval Art*, 2nd ed. Boulder, CO: Westview Press, 2004. A survey of medieval art and architecture, including medieval castles. Art in context.

Stokstad, Marilyn, and Jerry Stannard. *Gardens of the Middle Ages*. Lawrence, KS: Spencer Museum of Art, University of Kansas, 1983. Includes gardens from all levels of society.

Zarnecki, George, Janet Holt, and Tristram Holland. *English Romanesque Art 1066–1200*. Hayward Gallery, London, April 5–July 8, 1984. London: Arts Council of Great Britain, 1984. The first of three exhibitions covering the years 1066–1547. Interpretive essays cover the period 1066–1200. See also Alexander and Marks.

Castles and Medieval Fortifications

Anderson, William. *Castles of Europe: From Charlemagne to the Renaissance*. Photographs by Wim Swaan. London: Elek, 1970. A general discussion with excellent images by one of the world's great architectural photographers.

Boase, T.S.R. *Castles and Churches of the Crusading Kingdom*. London and New York: Oxford University Press, 1967. The classic study of crusader architecture including both religious and secular architecture, travelers' accounts, and Jerusalem itself.

Brown, R. Allen. *The Architecture of Castles: A Visual Guide*. New York: Facts on File, 1984. A brief but useful survey.

———. *Castles from the Air*. Cambridge, UK, and New York: Cambridge University Press, 1989. Use of aerial photography in archeology. Excellent images; published in the series "Cambridge Air Surveys."

The Chateaux of France. Edited by Daniel Wheeler. An Hachette-Vendome Book. New York: Vendome Press, 1979. Primarily photographs; good, succinct introductions.

Colvin, Howard M., A. J. Talor, and R. A. Brown. *A History of the King's Works*. London: H.M. Stationary Office, 1963–82. A multivolume study with extensive documentation of buildings built and financed by kings.

Coulson, Charles L. *Castles in Medieval Society, Fortresses in England, France and Ireland in the Central Middle Ages*. Oxford: Oxford University Press, 2003. A new interpretation of castles as impressive residences and only secondarily as military architecture; a discussion of the role of women and children; extensive and thorough documentation.

Creighton, Oliver. *Castles and Landscapes*. London and New York: Continuum, 2002. A new approach to castles and their sites influenced by new studies in the history of landscape architecture; the impact of castles on the countryside.

Creighton, Oliver, and Robert Higham. *Medieval Castles*. Shire, 2003. A concise survey of castles of England and Wales, including a discussion of their residential and military functions, as seen in the archeology of the sites.

Emery, Anthony. *Greater Medieval Houses of England and Wales, 1300–1500*. Vol. 1, *Northern England*. Vol. 2, *East Anglia, Central England, and Wales*. Cambridge, UK: Cambridge University Press, 1996. Vol. 3 in progress. A comprehensive survey of English and Welsh houses, 1300–1500, including the history of the building and current research on the site; in the context of social history (e.g., the elite residence); biography (e.g., John of Gaunt); and includes pithy, thematic essays (e.g., the trophy house).

Erlande-Brandenburg, Alain. *Cathedrals and Castles, Building in the Middle Ages*, Discoveries Series. Translated by Rosemary Stonehewer. New York: Harry N. Abrams, 1995. Originally published by Gallimard, in Paris, 1993.

Fedden, Robin, and John Thomson. *Crusader Castles*. London: J. Murray, 1957. Includes some lesser-known examples.

Fernie, Eric. *The Architecture of Norman England*. Oxford: Oxford University Press, 2000. An excellent survey of the traditions and innovations of Norman architects in England; studies of individual building types such as castles, halls, and churches.

Gies, Joseph, and Frances Gies. *Life in a Medieval Castle*. New York: Harper & Row, 1979. Daily life as experienced in Chepstow Castle in Wales.

Higham, R., and P. Barker. *Timber Castles*. London: Batsford, 1992. A thorough discussion of an often overlooked subject.

Hindley, Geoffrey. *Castles of Europe*. Feltham, UK: Hamlyn, 1968. A comprehensive survey in the series "Great Buildings of the World."

Johnson, Matthew. *Behind the Castle Gate; From Medieval to Renaissance*. London and New York: Routledge, 2002. Reviews castle studies 1350–1600; joins the debate over military versus social use of castles; argues that castles built between 1350 and 1600 succeed as "stage settings"; relates castles to social function; close analysis of layout and use.

Johnson, Paul. *Castles of England, Scotland and Wales*. London: Seven Dials, 2000. An excellent concise survey, including eighteenth- and nineteenth-century neomedieval castles.

Kennedy, Hugh. *Crusader Castles*. Cambridge, UK: Cambridge University Press, 1994. The architecture and history of Christian crusader castles from 1099 to 1291; the castles of the Templars and Hospitalers; and a comparison with Muslim fortifications.

Kenyon, John R. *Medieval Fortifications*. Leicester: Leicester University Press, 1990.

Kenyon, John R., and Richard Avent, eds. *Castles in Wales and the Marches: Essays in Honour of Cathcart King*. Cardiff: University of Wales Press, 1987. Fortifications on the border between England and Wales.

King, D. J. Cathcart. *The Castle in England and Wales: An Interpretative History*. London: Croom Helm, 1988. Emphasis on the military aspects of English and Welsh castles, with special attention to problems of defense.

Le Page, Jean-Denis G. G. *Castles and Fortified Cities of Medieval Europe, an Illustrated History*. Jefferson, NC, and London: McFarland & Company, 2002. A chronological survey of castles and cities throughout Europe, including many unusual examples, illustrated with drawings by the author.

Liddiard, Robert, ed. *Anglo-Norman Castles*. Woodbridge, Suffolk, UK: Boydell Press, 2003. Nineteen important essays by leading scholars, including John Blair, R. Allen Brown, Majorie Chibnall, Charles Coulson, Richard Eales, and T. A. Heslop, in-depth studies that redefine the social and architectural history of castles from the eleventh century to the middle of the thirteenth century.

Macaulay, David. *Castle*. London: William Collins, Sons, 1977. Drawings illustrating construction; based on Harlech.

Mesqui, Jean. *Chateaux et Enceintes de la France Medievale*. 2 vols. Paris, 1991–93. Text in French; however, excellent drawings and photographs make this a useful reference work.

Molin, Kristian. *Unknown Crusader Castles*. New York and London: Hambledon and London, 2001. A comparison of the castles of the eastern Mediterranean including castles built in Cypres, Armenia, and Greece; includes military and nonmilitary uses of castles.

Morshead, Owen. *Windsor Castle*. 2nd rev. ed. London: Phaidon Press, 1957. A historical survey of a single castle with emphasis on social history.

Muller-Wiener, Wolfgang. *Castles of the Crusaders*. Photographs by A. F. Kersting. Translated from German by J. Maxwell Brownjohn. London: Thames and Hudson; New York and Toronto: McGraw-Hill Book Company, 1966. A broad survey, useful for its inclusion of castles in Greece.

Oman, Charles. *Castles*. New York: Beekman House, 1978. A classic study; this edition is based on the author's 1924–25 work.

Platt, Colin. *The Castle in Medieval England and Wales*. London: Secker & Warburg, 1982. The castle in its social context, 1066–1485 in England, to 1536 in Wales.

Pounds, N.J.G. *The Medieval Castle in England and Wales: A Social and Political History*. Cambridge, UK, and New York: Cambridge University Press, 1990. Social conditions, politics, and government, 1066–1485.

Renn, D. F. *Norman Castles in Britain*. London: John Baker Publishers; New York: Humanities Press, 1968. Brief historical overview, followed by a complete gazeteer, locating and describing in a unique code all the castles and remains of castles in the British Isles built before the reign of Henry III.

Reyerson, Cathryn, and Faye Poe, eds. *The Medieval Castle: Romance and Reality*. Medieval Studies at Minnesota. Dubuque, IA: Kendall/Hunt, 1984. Castles in literature and art.

Ritter, Raymond. *L'Architecture Militaire du Moyen Age*. Paris: Fayard, 1974. A very useful survey of French castles from the early Middle Ages to the Renaissance.

Ross, Susan. *The Castles of Scotland*. London: G. Philip, 1973.

Saalman, Howard. *Medieval Cities*, Planning and Cities. New York: George Braziller, 1968. A concise treatment of the character and development of medieval cities with many plans and prints.

Simpson, W. Douglas. *Castles in England and Wales*. London: Batsford, 1969. The origin, development, and decline of castles and the part they played in the history of the British Isles told in a readable literary style. Begins with Scott's *Ivanhoe* and enthusiasm for the Middle Ages; includes Penrhyn Castle and concludes with modern efforts at restoration.

Taylor, Arnold, ed. *The Welsh Castles of Edward I*. London: Ronceverte, WV: Hambledon Press, 1986. Originally published as Volume 1 and 2 of *History of the King's Works*, in 1963, a series emphasizing documentary history, edited by H. M. Colvin.

Taylor, Robert R. *The Castles of the Rhine, Recreating the Middle Ages in Modern Germany*. Waterloo, ON: Wilfrid Laurier University Press, 1998. A study of the political and economic implications of castles in their own time and for nineteenth- and twentieth-century Germany.

Thompson, A. Hamilton. *Military Architecture in England During the Middle Ages*. London: Henry Froude, Oxford University Press, 1912. An excellent early attempt to write a systematic history of castles from a military point of view; includes extensive quotations from original documents, illustrated with drawings and some photographs.

Thompson, Michael. *The Medieval Hall: The Basis of Secular Domestic Life, 600–1600 AD*. Aldershot, UK: Scolar Press; Brookfield, VT: Ashgate Publishing Co., 1995. The design and function of domestic architecture.

———. *The Rise of the Castle*. Cambridge, UK: Cambridge University Press, 1991. The origins of castle design, 449–1066; a social history.

Thompson, Michael Welman. *The Decline of the Castle*. Cambridge, UK, and New York: Cambridge University Press, 1987. Sequel to *The Rise of the Castle*. Surveys the period of 1485–1714.

Toy, Sidney. *A History of Fortification from 3000 B.C. to A.D. 1700*. New York: Macmillan, 1955. The standard history of castles, fortifications, and sieges.

Tuulse, Armin. *Castles of the Western World*. Translated by R. P. Girdwood. London: Thames and Hudson, 1958. Survey of the castles of Europe; with an emphasis on military aspects of castles; many useful plans and reconstruction drawings and black-and-white photographs; includes lesser known castles in Switzerland, Low Countries, Scandinavia, and Finland as well as England, France, Italy, and Germany.

Warner, Philip. *The Medieval Castle; Life in a Fortress in Peace and War.* London: Barker, 1971. A volume in the series "Medieval Life." The art and science of war.

Woolgar, C. M. *The Great Household in Late Medieval England.* New Haven: Yale University Press, 1999. A recent social study; invaluable for an understanding of the uses of castles and the requirements of castle design; carefully documented.

Films

Snow White and the Seven Dwarfs. 1938. Director: David Hand. Walt Disney's first full-length animated film; the castle was inspired by the castle (alcazar) of Segovia; Disney received a special Oscar for the film.

Henry V. 1944. Director: Laurence Olivier. Cast: Laurence Olivier, Robert Newton, Leslie Banks. Shakespeare's play as interpreted by Laurence Olivier; filled with colorful pageantry; the charge of the French knights at Agincourt is memorable; Olivier won an honorary Oscar for acting, directing, and producing this film. Highly stylized architecture.

Ivanhoe. 1952. Director: Richard Thorpe. Cast: Robert Taylor, Elizabeth Taylor, Joan Fontaine, George Sanders. Based on the novel by Sir Walter Scott; a classic swashbuckler. Ivanhoe must gain Richard the Lion Hearted's release from captivity and protect the Fair Maidens—Taylor and Fontaine—from George Sanders at his evil best. The castles are as fanciful as the characters.

Richard III. 1955. Director: Laurence Olivier. Cast: Laurence Olivier, Ralph Richardson, John Gielgud, Claire Bloom. Shakespeare's play as interpreted by Laurence Olivier; Olivier makes Richard one of the nastiest villains of all time.

Becket. 1964. Director: Peter Glenville. Cast: Richard Burton, Peter O'Toole. Depicts the stormy and finally violent relationship between Henry II and the archbishop of Canterbury, Thomas à Becket. Some good architectural recreations.

The Lion in Winter. 1968. Adapted by James Goldman from his play. Director: Anthony Harvey. Cast: Katharine Hepburn, Peter O'Toole, Anthony Hopkins. The conflict between Henry II and Eleanor of Aquitaine; Hepburn won an Oscar for her interpretation of Eleanor; the castle settings are unusually accurate.

Henry V. 1989. Director: Kenneth Branagh. Cast: Kenneth Branagh, Derek Jacobi, Paul Scofield, Judi Dench, Ian Holm, Emma Thompson. Shakespeare's play interpreted by Branagh as an epic bloody struggle. A realistic view of medieval warfare.

Braveheart. 1995. Director: Mel Gibson. Cast: Mel Gibson, Sophie Marceau, Patrick McGoohen. William Wallace fights Edward I for Scotland in an epic re-creation of the period, the battles, and the horrors.

The Crusades. 1995. Directors: Alan Ereira and David Wallace. Cast: Terry Jones. Made for A & E, 4-tape set. Monty Python's complete history of the Crusades with medievalist Terry Jones as host. Funny and educational at the same time.

The story of Robin Hood has become a film industry. The castles are fanciful and spectacular, but have little resemblance to castles of the twelfth century—the period of Richard the Lion Hearted and Robin Hood. Watch for all the mistakes in castle design made by the producers.
Some of the best—and funniest—productions are:

Robin Hood. 1923. Director Allan Dwan. Cast: Douglas Fairbanks Jr., Enid Bennett, Wallace Barry. The archetype of all swashbuckler films; from the silent film era. No castle had such stairs and wall hangings.

Robin and Marian. 1976. Director: Richard Lester. Cast: Sean Connery, Audrey Hepburn, Richard Harris. Another great swashbuckler.

Robin Hood: Prince of Thieves. 1991. Director: Kevin Reynolds. Cast: Kevin Costner, Sean Connery, Morgan Freeman, Mary Elizabeth Mastrantonio, Alan Rickman. A retelling notable for the addition of a Moorish warrior to assist Robin.

BBC Productions in 1986 made *Robin Hood: The Swords of Wayland* and *Robin Hood: Herne's Son.* Other versions of Robin Hood were made in 1973 and 1991.

Comic possibilities are exploited in Mel Brooks' *Robin Hood: Men in Tights* (1991), *Robin and the Seven Hoods* (a musical with Frank Sinatra, 1964), and *Robin Hood of Locksley* (a modern Robin Hood becomes a computer hacker, 1996).

Web Sites

http://www.castles-abbeys.co.uk   Castles, Abbeys and Medieval Buildings: photos and good essays on a number of sites in the United Kingdom.

http://www.castles-of-britain.com   Castles of Britain: a site sponsored by Castles Unlimited, an organization dedicated to preserving the castles in Britain and promoting their study.

http://www.castlesontheweb.com   Castles on the Web: many links to photos, books, and preservation organizations.

http://www.castleswales.com/hom.html   Castles of Wales: an excellent site with maps, reference materials, and historical essays. Has a good section on "Life in a Medieval Castle."

http://www.castlexplorer.co.uk/   CastleXplorer: a colorful and informational site designed for tourists.

http://www.eropamedievale.it   Medieval Europe Search Engine: a mega-site with many links.

http://www.greatcastlesofwales.co.uk   The Great Castles of Wales: many photos and plans on a site mainly pitched at castle tourism.

http://www.medieval-life.net   Medieval Life: very good essays on clothing, food, festivals, chivalry, and other aspects of medieval life directed at the non-specialist.

http://www.netserf.org   NetSERF: The Internet Connection for Medieval Resources, a mega-site with links to almost everything about the Middle Ages, including castles.

INDEX

About the Author

MARILYN STOKSTAD is Judith Harris Murphy Distinguished Professor of Art History emerita at the University of Kansas, Lawrence, and consultative curator of medieval art at the Nelson-Atkins Museum of Art in Kansas City, Missouri. She is the author of the textbooks, *Art History* (1995, 2005), *Art: A Brief History* (2000, 2004), and *Medieval Art* (1986, 2004). Her scholarly work includes studies on twelfth-century sculpture, medieval gardens, and the pilgrimage to Santiago de Compostela. She has also served as a consultant to the St. Louis Art Museum, the *World Book Encyclopedia*, and several major book publishers.